# Trade Blocs: Economics and Politics

Preferential trade blocs are in vogue. Despite the successes achieved in liberalizing trade by multilateral trade negotiations sponsored by the World Trade Organization (WTO), numerous countries have separately negotiated preferential trade treaties with one another. Representing a significant departure from the WTO's central principle of non-discrimination among member countries, preferential trade blocs are now the subject of an intense academic and policy debate. The first section of this book presents a rudimentary and intuitive introduction to the economics of preferential trade agreements. The following chapters present the author's theoretical and empirical research on a number of questions surrounding the issue of preferential trade agreements, including the design of necessarily welfare-improving trade blocs, the quantitative (econometric) evaluation of the economic (welfare) impact of preferential trade liberalization, and the impact of preferential trade agreements and the multilateral trade system.

PRAVIN KRISHNA is Chung Ju Yung Professor of International Economics at Johns Hopkins University and Faculty Research Fellow of the National Bureau of Economic Research. He was previously Professor of Economics at Brown University and has held visiting appointments at the University of Chicago, Princeton University, and Stanford University. Professor Krishna has also served as a consultant to the World Bank and the International Monetary Fund.

# Trade Blocs:
# Economics and Politics

——✢——

**Pravin Krishna**

*Johns Hopkins University*

CAMBRIDGE UNIVERSITY PRESS
Cambridge, New York, Melbourne, Madrid, Cape Town, Singapore, São Paulo

Cambridge University Press
40 West 20th Street, New York, NY 10011-4211, USA

www.cambridge.org
Information on this title: www.cambridge.org/9780521770668

First published 2005

Printed in the United States of America

*A catalog record for this publication is available from the British Library.*

*Library of Congress Cataloging in Publication Data*
Krishna, Pravin.
Trade blocs : economics and politics / Pravin Krishna.
p.   cm. – (Japan-U.S. Center UFJ Bank monographs on international
financial markets)
Includes bibliographical references and index.
ISBN 0-521-77066-1 (hardcover)
1. Trade blocs – Econometric models.   2. International trade – Econometric
models.   3. Protectionism – Econometric models.   I. Title.   II. Series.
HF1418.7.K75   2005
382′.9 – dc22        2005004040

ISBN-13   978-0-521-77066-8 hardback
ISBN-10   0-521-77066-1 hardback

# Contents

Contents

# Contents

# Figures

# Tables

# Acknowledgments

In the last decade, much academic and policy attention has been focused on how to design institutions that would induce nations toward the widely held ideal of global free trade. Given the rapid proliferation of preferential trading agreements (PTAs) both implemented and proposed in this period, it is not surprising that much of this discussion centered on the desirability of preferential trading. Many old questions relating to the economic consequences of preferential trade blocs have been revisited, and several new questions have emerged concerning the impact of trade blocs on the multilateral trade system. This book presents the results of some of my research on these questions.

Although I have accumulated many intellectual debts in the course of this work, I am especially beholden to Jagdish Bhagwati, who first turned my attention to the issue of preferential trading blocs while I was still a graduate student at Columbia University. His insights, energy, and support provided much inspiration then and continue to do so today. I am most grateful as well to Arvind Panagariya, from whose mastery of preferential trade theory I learned so much during the course of our joint work in this area.

I gratefully acknowledge the support of the Sanwa Bank for its promotion of the Sanwa Bank Monograph Program. I am particularly indebted to Professor Ryuzo Sato and Professor Rama Ramachandran at the Center for Japan–U.S. Business and Economic Studies at New York University (NYU) for their advice and encouragement. For helpful comments and suggestions on the research described in this book, I am grateful to Ritu Basu, Jagdish Bhagwati, Robert Feenstra, Ronald Findlay, Andrew Foster, Kishore Gawande, Jim Harrigan, Elhanan Helpman, Tom Krebs, Lawrence Lau, John McLaren, Devashish Mitra, Arvind Panagariya, Jim Rauch, Dani Rodrik, Bent Sorensen, Mazen Soueid, David Weil, Alan Winters and to seminar participants at Brown, UC Berkeley, UC Irvine, UCLA, UC San Diego, UC Santa Barbara, UC Santa Cruz, the University of Chicago, Columbia, Dartmouth, Florida International University, Georgetown, Harvard, the International Monetary Fund (IMF), the Inter-American Development Bank, NYU,

## Acknowledgments

Northwestern, Stanford, and Yale. I am also grateful to Joseph Hebr at the U.N. Statistics Division and Patricia Burke at U.S. Customs for their help in putting the data together, and to Sajjid Chinoy, Mike Robbins, Vicharee Vichit-Vadakan, and Narayanan Subramanian for superb research assistance. The analysis of PTAs presented herein draws directly on research that has been published in a number of peer-reviewed journals, including the *Journal of Political Economy, Quarterly Journal of Economics,* and *Journal of International Economics,* whose editors and referees made many valuable suggestions on methodology and content for which I am very grateful. Finally, George Stergios edited the manuscript with great care, and I am greatly indebted to him for his many excellent suggestions on the exposition.

Brown University was my home institution for the last several years (1995–2004). During the course of this research, I also spent a year (1997–1998) at Stanford University, took up an appointment as John Olin Visiting Professor at the University of Chicago (2000–2001), and spent another year (2002–2003) as Visiting Fellow at the International Economics Section at Princeton University. These were all very stimulating research environments and I remain most grateful for their intellectual and financial support and for their hospitality.

# CHAPTER ONE

# Introduction and Overview

## 1.1  Objectives

**P**referential trade agreements (PTAs) are now in vogue. Even as multilateral approaches to trade liberalization – through negotiations organized by the Geneva-based multilateral organization, the General Agreement on Tariffs and Trade (GATT), and its more recent incarnation, the World Trade Organization (WTO) – have made progress in reducing international barriers to trade, various countries have recently negotiated separate preferential trade treaties with each other in the form of GATT-sanctioned Free Trade Areas (FTAs) and Customs Unions (CUs). Among the more prominent are the North American Free Trade Agreement (NAFTA) and the MERCOSUR (the CU among the Argentine Republic, Brazil, Paraguay, and Uruguay).

Although by no means historically exceptional, this widespread implementation of PTAs does contrast strongly with the recent history of international trade relations. After the establishment in 1945 of the International Trade Organization (the ur-GATT) as a multilateral forum for trade-policy negotiations, few preferential treaties were initiated in the early post-war period. The European Community (EC), established subsequent to the 1957 Treaty of Rome, was a nearly singular exception with few successful imitators.

Many observers have argued that GATT negotiations were making such inroads on trade barriers during the early post-war period that PTAs fell out of fashion. In the period 1945–1975, trade barriers were reduced substantially through several multilateral negotiation rounds, each involving a growing number of member countries. This success has itself been attributed to a fundamental principle of the GATT: non-discrimination. Non-discrimination (as implied by the infelicitously labeled Most Favored Nation [MFN] clause of the GATT) requires that import duties applied by a country shall not depend on the partner from which an import originates. When combined with the reciprocity usually demanded in trade negotiations (where tariff reductions by one country are expected to be matched by tariff reductions by the partner countries), non-discrimination proved to be an extraordinarily useful lever in opening the doors to free trade. Non-discrimination obliges countries that reduce tariffs to apply the reductions to imports from all member countries; reciprocity, in turn, obliges those countries to provide matching tariff reductions. Together, they generated increasing momentum toward a complete dismantling of trade barriers.

However, this success with multilateral negotiations did not continue for long. The evident weaknesses of the GATT's dispute-settlement mechanisms, the exclusion of important sectors of the economy (e.g., agriculture, textiles, and the increasingly important services sector) from its ambit, and the proliferation of new and more complex instruments of trade protection (e.g., anti-dumping procedures) that enabled countries to effectively sidestep GATT agreements led, by the 1980s, to numerous calls for the extension and reinforcement of the system. A number of countries turned to bilateral (i.e., preferential) arrangements. The GATT's Uruguay Round of trade negotiations, concluded in 1994, created the WTO and the GATT itself (now expanded to finally include agriculture and textiles, *inter alia*) was folded into the WTO's mandate. The Uruguay Round also gave the WTO two other agreements to oversee: the General Agreements on Trade in Services (GATS) and the agreement on Trade Related Intellectual Property Rights (TRIPS). Important changes to strengthen the dispute-settlement process and to make it more efficient were implemented. However, the interest in PTAs did not wane; several dozen additional agreements were signed in the 1990s and several more are now under consideration.

This renewed tendency toward preferential trading has led to a parallel revival of academic and policy interest in the *desirability* of such agreements. Although even seasoned analysts in the popular press and in policy circles have mistakenly equated free-trade agreements with free trade, it is well understood by specialists, at least since the classic analysis of Viner (1950), that, in contrast to the more popular notion that freer trade is economically improving ("welfare-improving" in academic parlance), discriminatory liberalization may in fact be economically worsening ("welfare-reducing") for the liberalizing country. These theoretical possibilities make the economics of PTAs unusually complex and interesting. In recent discussions on PTAs, the question of the welfare impact of PTAs has been revisited and reexamined in a number of different ways. Several new issues have been raised and addressed as well, including the following:

- How can welfare-improving PTAs that eliminate the possibility of welfare loss for both member countries and non-members be designed? How do the political desires of governments (e.g., to shield workers in particular industrial sectors or maintain the level of output in others) interfere with the problem of designing welfare-improving PTAs?
- Which types of PTAs are most likely to result in welfare improvement? In the face of the possibility of welfare reduction with preferential trading, the question has arisen as to whether we can identify any country characteristics that make economic improvement rather than worsening the likelier outcome. Following the analysis of Viner (1950), a number of prominent analysts attempted in the early 1960s to theoretically identify country characteristics that would render unlikely adverse outcomes. Nevertheless, much of the early research on this topic (notably Meade [1955], Lipsey [1958, 1960], Johnson [1962], and a later synthesis by McMillan and McCann [1980]) yielded results that were generally considered mostly taxonomic and of limited practical applicability and operational significance. In this context, a number of influential analysts (e.g., Wonnacott and Lutz [1987], Krugman [1991], and Summers [1991]) have suggested

a criterion that is remarkably simple and whose implementation would perhaps only require the most readily
available data: geographic proximity. They have argued
that we should encourage PTAs between geographically
proximate countries over PTAs with distant ones because
the former are more likely to avoid the adverse possibility
of welfare reduction and to lead to a larger improvement
in welfare. Preferential trade between the geographically
proximate has thus been argued to be "natural." But, do
regional (i.e., geographically proximate) countries indeed
make for "natural" trading partners in the context of preferential trading? Or is there no basis for "regionalism" in
preferential trade?

• What is the impact of bilateral agreements between countries on the multilateral trading system? The recent academic literature has been substantially concerned with
the issue of the impact of PTAs on the multilateral system symbolized by the GATT/WTO. This is because preferential trade treaties, although sanctioned by the GATT
(under Article XXIV), stand as an exception to the GATT's
own fundamental principle of non-discrimination, thus
raising the question of whether such discriminatory arrangements undermine the multilateral framework under
which so much success had been achieved in liberalizing

trade. What are the incentives faced by member countries in a PTA for further multi-lateral liberalization? Are trade blocs, indeed, stepping stones toward multilateral free trade? Or will they instead inhibit multilateral progress?

This monograph presents results from my research on a number of these issues and places them in the context of ongoing discussions on these topics.[1]

## 1.2 Outline and Summary of Major Results

The book is organized as follows. Chapter 2 outlines the basic economics of PTAs. This treatment is intended to provide a rudimentary and intuitive background to the issues that this book addresses and is aimed at readers without any previous exposure to the analytics of PTAs. In particular, the central idea regarding the possibility of welfare reduction with PTAs is developed in detail. This provides an intuitive foundation for the analysis that follows in subsequent chapters.

Chapter 3 discusses the design of welfare-improving PTAs that ensure gains for member countries without negatively impacting outsiders. We introduce first the classic analysis

---

[1] See Bhagwati (1993), Panagariya (2000), and Schiff and Winters (2003) for survey discussions.

of Kemp and Wan (1976), which provided an extraordinarily simple theoretical solution to this problem for the
case of CUs. Then, after discussing the problems inherent
in extending the Kemp–Wan solution to the case of the
more popular type of PTA – the free trade agreement (in
which countries retain their right to independent external
tariff policies) – the recent result of Panagariya and Krishna
(2002), which nevertheless develops a welfare-improving
FTA solution analogous to that of Kemp and Wan (1976),
is described in detail. The design of welfare-improving PTAs
in the presence of additional "non-economic" constraints,
which draws on the work of Krishna and Bhagwati (1997),
is also described. Finally, practical and institutional issues
that arise in the implementation of such necessarily welfare-
improving PTAs are discussed.

Chapter 4 describes the analysis of Krishna (2003a) of
the putative role of geography in preferential trade. It starts
by discussing the arguments made by Krugman (1991) and
others in support of regionalism in preferential trade. Then,
a simple theoretical framework is developed that serves as
a platform for empirical investigation of this issue. Specifically, expressions for the welfare change that would result when one country preferentially reduces tariffs against
any partner are derived and the parameters that need to be

estimated to assess welfare change with preferential tariff reduction are identified. A strategy to investigate the merits of a policy of regionalism is then discussed. This involves the use of trade data of a country to estimate the relevant parameters and obtain assessments of the potential welfare effects that would result from preferential reduction in tariffs by that country on imports from various geographically dispersed potential partner countries, and to then examine correlations between these estimates of the overall welfare effects with the distance of the partner countries from the home country. The econometric methodology is described in detail. Finally, Chapter 4 presents empirical results obtained using data on trade flows from the United States. The findings, however, are in the negative. Distance is not found to be significantly related to welfare change with preferential trade reduction.

Chapter 5 departs from the "static" analysis of PTAs and moves on instead to what Bhagwati (1993) has called the "dynamic" or "time-path" question where, instead of single or one-step arrangements, the successive *expansion* of existing PTAs to include ever more countries is considered. Are there incentives for FTAs to keep expanding with more members so as to move toward multilateral free trade eventually, or will there be incentives instead to keep new

members out? This question regarding the potential interaction between bilateralism and multilateralism has been a
dominant issue in the recent revival of interest in PTAs, with
one popular contention being that PTAs offered a faster way
to global free trade than did multilateral approaches. The results of Krishna (1998) — which argue that PTAs reduce the
incentives for multilateral liberalization, sometimes rendering infeasible previously feasible movements to global free
trade — are developed and discussed along with other recent
contributions in this area.

— ✝ CHAPTER TWO ✝ —

# The Economics of Preferential Trade Areas

A cornerstone of the Geneva-based multilateral organization, the GATT, and its more recent incarnation, the WTO, is the principle of non-discrimination: Member countries may not discriminate against goods entering their borders based on the country of origin. However, in a nearly singular exception to its own central prescript, the WTO does permit its members to enter into PTAs, provided these preferences are complete — thereby sanctioning the formation of FTAs, whose members are obligated to eliminate internal import barriers, and CUs, whose members additionally agree on a common external tariff against imports from non-members.[1] Such PTAs are now in vogue. Even as multilateral

[1] More specifically, FTAs and CUs may be formed under Article XXIV of the GATT, which permits PTAs provided that trade barriers between members are eliminated on substantially all trade (i.e., the

approaches to trade liberalization — through negotiations organized by the GATT/WTO — have made substantial progress in reducing international barriers to trade, various countries have negotiated separate preferential trade treaties with each other in the form of GATT/WTO–sanctioned PTAs. Among the more prominent PTAs currently in existence are NAFTA, the European Economic Community (EEC), and the MERCOSUR (i.e., the CU between the Argentine Republic, Brazil, Paraguay, and Uruguay).[2]

That a country entering an FTA (where it eliminates tariffs against select partners) is doing something distinct from free trade as such (where it eliminates tariffs against all imports regardless of country of origin) should be easy to see. What this implies for the liberalizing country is a little more

preferences are complete). Additional exceptions to the GATT's principle of non-discrimination include the Enabling Clause, which permits developing countries to grant to each other whatever preferences to which they may agree, and the Generalized System of Preferences, which allows developed countries to grant preferential access to developing countries. Both Article XXIV and the Enabling Clause are discussed in Appendix 2.1.

[2] It is perhaps worth pointing out that NAFTA and the EEC were formed under Article XXIV of the GATT and that MERCOSUR, on the other hand, was formed under the Enabling Clause referred to previously. A complete list of PTAs reported to the GATT to date is provided in Appendix 2.2.

difficult to understand. Even a good half-century after the economic implications of FTAs were first articulated by Viner (1950), the differences between FTAs and free trade remain a nuance that most policy analysts (and, occasionally, distinguished economists) appear to miss. So, how is the economics of free trade agreement different from that of free trade? And what does this distinction imply for the conduct of economic policy?

A thorough answer to these questions would require the reader to take a deep plunge into the abstruse theoretical world of the "second-best," whose existence and complexities were, indeed, first discovered and developed by analysts working on the economics of PTAs.[3] Under the safe presumption that the enthusiasm for the mysteries of second-best worlds on the part of most readers will not match our own, we introduce the idea first in a rudimentary fashion using the following "textbook" representation of Viner's

---

[3] Whereas elimination of *all* economic distortions can be shown to be welfare-improving, a second-best situation is characterized by some unremoved distortions in whose presence the elimination of some other distortions may be welfare-decreasing. In the context of PTAs, the eliminated distortions are the tariff barriers against PTA partners; the unremoved distortions are the trade barriers against imports from the rest of the world. See Lipsey and Lancaster (1957) for a classic treatment of second-best analysis, and Krishna and Panagariya (2000) for a more recent generalization.

analysis. Consider the case of three countries, A, B, and C, where A is the "home" country. A produces a good and trades it for imports from its partners B and C. Initially, imports from B and C are subject to non-discriminatory trade restrictions: tariffs against B and C are equal. Imagine now that A eliminates its tariffs against B (as part of a free trade agreement, say) while maintaining its tariffs against C. This is a preferential tariff reduction as opposed to free trade because the latter would require that tariffs against C be removed as well. It is tempting to think that this reduction of tariffs against B is a step in the direction of free trade and, therefore, that this ought to deliver to country A a proportionate fraction of the benefits of complete free trade. However, Viner (1950) showed that this need not (and generally would not) be the case. Indeed, whereas a complete move toward free trade would be welfare-improving for country A, Viner demonstrated that the tariff preference granted to B through the free trade agreement could, in fact, worsen A's welfare.

## 2.1 Trade Creation and Trade Diversion

Figures 2.1 and 2.2 illustrate preferential tariff reform as welfare-enhancing and welfare-worsening, respectively.

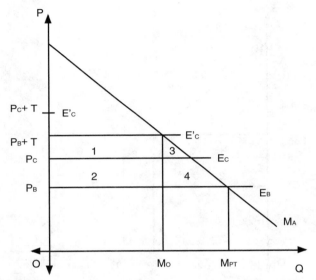

**Figure 2.1** *Trade-Creating Tariff Preferences: Change in Welfare =* *(3+4)*

The y-axes denote price and the x-axes denote quantities. $M_A$ denotes the import demand curve of country A. $E_B$ and $E_C$ denote the price at which countries B and C are willing to supply A's demand; they represent the export supply curves of B and C, respectively. In Figure 2.1, B is assumed to be a more efficient supplier of A's import than is C: $E_B$ is drawn below $E_W$, and its export price $P_B$ is less than C's export price $P_C$. Let $T$ denote the non-discriminatory per-unit tariff that

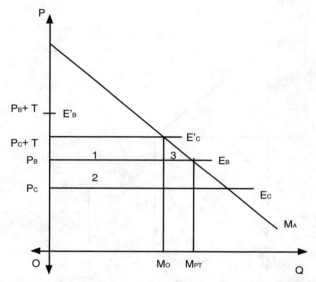

**Figure 2.2** *Trade-Diverting Tariff Preferences: Change in Welfare =*
*(3−2)*

is applied against B and C. This renders the tariff-inclusive price to importers in A as $P_B + T$ and $P_C + T$, respectively. With this non-discriminatory tariff in place, imports initially equal $M_0$ and the good is entirely imported from B. Tariff revenues in this initial situation equal the areas (1+2). When tariffs against B are eliminated preferentially, imports rise to $M_{PT}$. Imports continue to come entirely from B (because the import price from B now, $P_B$, is lower than the tariff-inclusive price of imports from C, $P_C + T$). The tariff preferences granted to B simply increase the volume of imports. This increase in the volume of trade with the country whose exports were initially being purchased by A anyway (i.e., with the more efficient producer) when tariffs against it are preferentially reduced is referred to as "trade creation," which can be shown here to be welfare-improving. The increase in benefit to consumers (i.e., consumer surplus) in A following the reduction in consumption prices from $P_B + T$ to $P_B$ equals the areas (1+2+3+4). No tariff revenue is now earned so the loss of tariff revenue equals areas (1+2). The overall gain to A from this preferential tariff reduction equals areas (1+2+3+4) − (1+2) = areas (3+4), a positive number. Thus, the trade-creating tariff preference is welfare-improving.

In demonstrating that the tariff preference considered is welfare-improving for the home country, A, we assumed that the partner that receives this tariff preference, B, is the more efficient supplier of the good. Figure 2.2 reverses this assumption, making C, the rest of the world, the more efficient supplier of the good. $E_C$ is therefore drawn below $E_B$. Initial imports are $M_0$. The tariff revenue collected is equal to the areas (1+2). When tariffs are eliminated against B, the less efficient partner, the tariff-inclusive price of imports from C is higher than the tariff-exclusive price from B (this need not necessarily be the case; it is simply so as drawn). This implies that all trade is now "diverted" away from C to B. What is the welfare consequence of this trade diversion? The increase in consumer surplus is equal to the areas (1+3) because consumers now pay a price equal to $P_B$ for this good. The loss in tariff revenue is (1+2). The overall gain to A equals the area (3−2), which may or may not be positive. Thus, a trade-diverting tariff preference may lead to a welfare reduction.

The preceding examples illustrate well the central issues emphasized in the academic literature on the welfare consequences of preferential trading. PTAs that create trade increase welfare; PTAs that divert trade *may* reduce welfare. In more general contexts, with more than one commodity imported, this idea may be extended and modified: Preferential tariff reduction on a basket of imports from a particular partner country will result in some trade creation and some trade diversion and, loosely speaking, the welfare of the liberalizing country is lowered if trade creation is dominated by trade diversion.[4] Absent any further information regarding

---

[4] It should be emphasized that we are only speaking in the loosest terms here. A formal treatment of this "trade-off" is deferred until a later chapter.

the particulars of the economies being considered, the outcome of preferential tariff reductions with regard to the welfare of the liberalizing country is uncertain.

## 2.2 Revenue-Transfer Effects

Thus far, we have considered the case in which the home country is small relative to both the partner country and the rest of the world. In the Vinerian analysis illustrated in Figures 2.1 and 2.2 — with the exportable from the partner and the rest of the world being perfect substitutes — when consumption is switched from the rest of the world to the partner country, the partner country is assumed to be able to satisfy all of the home country's demand. What happens if B is so small that after receiving the tariff preference from A, it is unable to satisfy all of A's demand for its importable? This implies that A continues to import some amount from the rest of the world C (which we assume for the moment is so large that it is able to handle all of the changes in A's demand without letting this affect its supply price), even after granting preferential access to B.

Here, it can be shown that the home country loses unambiguously, illustrated in the following example, provided by Panagariya (2000). In Figure 2.3, the export supply curve of

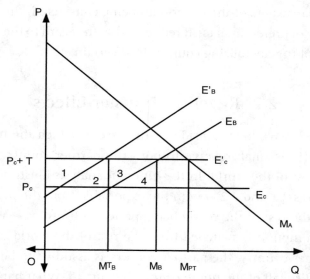

**Figure 2.3** *Revenue-Transfer Effects: Change in Welfare for Home =* $-(1+2+3+4)$; *Change in Welfare for Partner* $= (1+2+3)$; *Change in Welfare for Union* $= -(4)$

country B is shown to be rising. The tariff-inclusive supply curve faced by the home country is $E_B^T$. Total consumption of the importable initially is $M_0$ and imports from B are $M_B^T$. A tariff preference in favor of B simply shifts the effective export supply curve to $E_B$ and the imports from B to $M_B$. Total imports stay at $M_0$. The domestic price of the importable in the home market in A is set by C (which continues to supply to A) and is the same as before (i.e., it stays at $E_C^T$). The outcomes in this case are quite stark. Because consumption of the importable continues to be at $M_0$, there is no change in consumer surplus in the home country. There is, however, a direct tariff revenue loss because no tariff revenue is now earned on imports from the partner. The loss in tariff revenue (which is equal to the overall loss to A) equals the areas (1+2+3+4). In what can effectively be seen as a tariff revenue transfer to B, a gain of areas (1+2+3) accrues to B in the form of an increase in producer surplus. Thus, preferential tariff liberalization leads to a loss in welfare for the liberalizing country, a (smaller) gain in welfare for its partner, and a net loss of area (4) to the CU as a whole.

In the context of an *exchange* in tariff preferences negotiated under a PTA, once again we may expect that tariff revenue losses to the home country in some sectors are made up for by gains in other sectors in which the home country gets preferential access to its partner's markets. Who gains more will depend on the extent of tariff preferences exchanged and specific market circumstances (i.e., shapes of the supply and demand curves). The outcome is uncertain.[5]

---

[5] Also, we have not considered the possibility that there may be extra-union terms of trade effects. As the analysis of Mundell (1964) has shown, allowing for extra-union terms-of-trade effects may

We have so far studied the economic implications and income redistribution effects that follow a PTA between countries. The broadest message to retain from this discussion is
that welfare gains with preferential trading are highly ambiguous. Member countries may gain or lose with a PTA.
Moreover, although we have not explicitly considered this
so far, it should be easy to see that the rest of the world
may lose as well if demand for their exports by the member
countries in the PTA drops sufficiently so as to lower their
world prices (i.e., worsen their terms of trade with respect to
the rest of the world). It is worth noting, however, that the
ambiguous welfare outcomes have resulted from trade preferences that have taken quite specific forms. In particular,
we have analyzed tariff reductions in favor of the partner
while external tariffs against all outside countries are maintained at their initial levels. An important question relating
to institutional design can now be asked: By departing from
this particular structure of trade preferences, is it possible to
design PTAs in which welfare improvement for all countries
is guaranteed? It is to this topic that we turn next.

complicate matters further: the terms of trade of the tariff-reducing
country with respect to the rest of the world may rise or fall following a preferential reduction in its tariffs against a particular partner.
On this point, see also the recent analysis of Panagariya (1997).

# CHAPTER THREE

# Necessarily Welfare-Improving Preferential Trade Areas

I n the previous chapter, we developed in some detail the basic economics of PTAs. In particular, we argued that clear-cut answers with respect to the welfare impact of the formation of trading blocs between nations can rarely be obtained. A singular and important exception is the well-known result relating to CUs, stated independently by Kemp (1964) and Vanek (1965) and proved subsequently by Ohyama (1972) and Kemp and Wan (1976): Starting from a situation with an arbitrary structure of trade barriers, if two or more countries freeze their net external trade vector with the rest of the world through a set of common external tariffs and eliminate the barriers to internal trade (implying the formation of a CU), the welfare of the CU as a whole necessarily improves (weakly) and that of the rest of the world does not fall. A Pareto-improving PTA may thus be achieved. The Kemp–Wan construction offers a way to sidestep the complexities and ambiguities inherent in the analysis of PTAs and it has, therefore, played an important role in shaping the way that economists think about issues relating to the design and implementation of PTAs.

This chapter first discusses in detail this classic solution to the problem of designing welfare-improving CUs provided by Kemp and Wan (1976). After discussing the problems inherent in extending the Kemp–Wan solution to the case of the more popular type of PTA – the free-trade agreement (in which countries retain their right to independent external tariff policies) – the recent contribution of Panagariya and Krishna (2002), which nevertheless develops a welfare-improving free-trade agreement solution, analogous to that of Kemp and Wan (1976), is described. The design of welfare-improving PTAs in the presence of additional "non-economic" objectives, drawing on the work of Bhagwati and Krishna (1996), is also discussed. Finally, practical and institutional issues that arise in the implementation of such necessarily welfare-improving PTAs are discussed.[6]

---

[6] Much of the discussion on the topic of necessarily welfare-improving PTAs that follows draws heavily from Panagariya and

## 3.1 Customs Unions

The logic behind the design of the welfare-improving CU is as follows: By fixing the combined, net extra-union trade vector of member countries at its pre-union level, we can guarantee non-members (i.e., the rest of the world) their original level of welfare. Moreover, taking the extra-union trade vector as an endowment, the joint welfare of the CU is maximized by allowing free trade of goods internally (thus, in economics parlance, equating the marginal rate of substitution and marginal rate of transformation for each pair of commodities to each other and across all agents in the CU). It should be easy to see that the PTA thus constructed has a common internal price vector implying further a common external tariff; it is, therefore, a necessarily welfare-improving CU.

A simple proof of the Kemp–Wan result demonstrating the possibility of Pareto-improving CUs runs as follows.[7] We

Krishna (2002), Krishna and Bhagwati (1997), and Krishna (2003). Readers are referred to these papers for more comprehensive treatments.

[7] The formal proof outlined here on the design of welfare-improving CU is borrowed from Panagariya and Krishna (2002) and is somewhat different from the one presented by Kemp and Wan – although, as will be quite clear, the underlying logic remains entirely the same as the one used by Kemp and Wan. As will also become clear from

continue to consider our trading world with the home and partner countries, A and B, and the rest of the world, W. Using lower-case and upper-case letters to denote the home and the partner country, respectively, we let e(.) and E(.) denote the standard expenditure functions, and r(.) and R(.) the standard revenue functions. Consumer price vectors are denoted by p and P and welfare levels by u and U. An arbitrary structure of trade barriers may be assumed initially. The Kemp–Wan CU assumes that the total trade vector between the member countries and the rest of the world, W, is frozen; thus, the terms of trade with the rest of the world are the same in the CU equilibrium as initially. We are interested in showing that the joint utility of the home and the partner country is (weakly) greater in the CU equilibrium we construct and that the welfare of the rest of the world is the same as it is initially.

The income-expenditure inequality for the CU as a whole in the post-CU equilibrium is:

$$e(p^f, u^f) + E(P^f, U^f) = r(p^f) + R(P^f) + (p^f - P_W^o) m^o$$
$$+ (P^f - P_W^o) M^o \qquad (1)$$

our discussion later, the Panagariya–Krishna framework allows a relatively easy extension to the case of FTAs, whereas the Kemp–Wan methodology does not.

where the superscripts $o$ and $f$ denote the original equilibrium and the final (i.e., post-CU) equilibria, respectively; $p^f = P^f$ is the common internal price vector with the CU; $m^o$ and $M^o$ are vectors of quantities imported by the home and the partner country, respectively, from the rest of the world (i.e., they do not include the initial imports from each other) initially and (by construction) in the post-CU equilibrium. We note that $m^o$ is defined to include any goods from W that may have entered home through the partner in the pre-CU equilibrium. That is, in fixing the external import vector of a member, we include in it any goods that may have been imported or exported indirectly through the partner. A similar statement applies to $M^o$. Vector $P^o_W$ is the world price vector in the post-FTA equilibrium, which coincides with the pre-CU equilibrium because we freeze the joint external trade vector of the member countries with the rest of the world at their pre-CU levels. By the definition of the expenditure function, we have:

$$e(p^f, u^o) + E(P^f, U^o) \leq p^f d^o + P^f D^o \tag{2}$$

where $d$ and $D$ denote domestic consumption. For the home country, domestic demand ($d^o$) is satisfied by domestic production ($x^o$), imports from the rest of the world ($m^o$), and imports from the partner country ($n^o$). The same is true for the partner country. Using the fact that $n^o = -N^o$ and that $P_W^o(m^o + M^o) = 0$ given trade balance between the member countries and the rest of the world, we have:

$$e(p^f, u^o) + E(P^f, U^o) \leq p^f x^o + P^f X^o$$
$$+ \left(P^f - P_W^o\right)(m^o + M^o) \quad (3)$$

For the joint welfare of the member countries to be greater in the CU equilibrium, it is sufficient that $e(p^f, u^f) + E(P^f, U^f) \geq e(p^f, u^o) + E(P^f, U^o)$. Note that (2) and (3) imply that for this to be true, we need that

$$r(p^f) + R(P^f) \geq p^f x^o + P^f X^o \quad (4)$$

which is trivially satisfied given the definition of the revenue function (i.e., because at the new prices, $p^F$ and $P^f$, domestic producers can at least continue to produce their original bundles and likely even do better). Thus, the joint welfare of the home and partner country in the CU equilibrium is greater than (or equal to) their initial level of welfare. Note that the common external tariff of the CU is the difference between the internal price vector $P^f = p^f$ and the external price vector $P_W^o$. This completes the proof.[8] The CU thus

[8] Because it is only the joint welfare of the CU countries that is improved by the formation of the CU, we need to rely on a system of lump-sum internal payments here to guarantee that *each* member

designed is a PTA in which non-members are just as well off as before and the welfare of the member countries is jointly higher (or at least no lower) than before.

### 3.1.1  Non-Economic Objectives

What if in the CU thus designed, member governments desire to maintain certain economic variables (e.g., the level of industrialization or factor employment in particular industries) at their pre-CU level? That a welfare-enhancing CU that achieved such an industrialization objective could still be designed was conjectured by Cooper and Massell (1965), Johnson (1965), and Bhagwati (1968). In an extension of the Kemp–Wan result, this was demonstrated formally by Krishna and Bhagwati (1997), who showed that, indeed, a wide variety of "non-economic" objectives could be accommodated within the CU without diminishing its Pareto-improving virtues. Thus, consider a situation where a member government desires the output of a particular industry in the CU equilibrium, say $x_i^f$, to be the same as the output of that industry in the pre-CU equilibrium, $x_i^o$. From the definition of the revenue function, we know that (4) still

country actually benefits from it. See, however, Grinols (1981), who derives a suitable scheme of internal payments that does not have this lump-sum feature and is based on pre-union observables.

holds. Given the same resources as before, producers are able to produce the same output in this industry as before and perhaps increase the value of overall output (given the new prices) by producing a different mix of goods in other industries than before. Indeed, by the same logic, even if the output constraint were imposed in *all* industries, (4) would not be violated. The government constraint may thus be satisfied while maintaining the (weakly) welfare-improving properties of the CU. It should easy to see that, given that the unconstrained outcome may be one where $x_i^f \neq x_i^o$, satisfaction of the output constraint in industry $i$ will likely require the use of a production tax or subsidy. That it is *optimal* to use such a *targeted* subsidy to achieve the desired objective within the Kemp–Wan CU, rather than through some other policy such as a change in the Kemp–Wan external tariff, is also demonstrated by Krishna and Bhagwati (1997).

As in Kemp and Wan (1976), consider a competitive world trading system with any number of countries and with no restrictions whatsoever on the initial tariffs of individual countries. Let any subset of countries form a CU. To see how aggregate gains for the member countries can be achieved, we use the familiar Samuelson (1956) social indifference curves, which enable us to write a well-behaved social-utility function. We allow for the use of lump-sum transfers between individuals in the member countries. This allows us to neglect distributional issues between the member countries and to assert that, as we move up to higher social-indifference curves, Pareto-superior outcomes can be achieved. The formulation of the problem closely parallels that of Bhagwati and Srinivasan (1969).

Let $i = 1.......n$ index goods and $j = 1.......J$ index member countries. Let the net import vector of the member countries from the rest of the world be denoted as $M = (M_1........M_n)$, where $M_i$ would be positive if the $i^{th}$ good was a net import from the rest of the world and negative if it was a net export. Following the Kemp–Wan design, we freeze the net import vector of the union at the pre-union level and maximize the social-utility function,

$$U = U(C_1.........C_n) \qquad (5)$$

subject to

$$C_i = \sum_j X_i^j \left( L_i^j, K_i^j \right) + M_i \ \forall \, i \qquad (6)$$

$$\sum_i L_i^j = L^j \ \forall \, j \qquad (7)$$

$$\sum_i K_i^j = K^j \ \forall \, j \qquad (8)$$

$$M_i = M_i^F \ \forall \, i \qquad (9)$$

where $C_i$ stands for aggregate availability of good $i$ in the union and $X_i^j$ stands for production in country $j$ of good $i$ using a factor combination of $L_i^j$ and $K_i^j$, respectively. $L^j$ and $K^j$ denote the total availability of these factors in country $j$. Although we only chose two factors of production, it will become clear that the results generalize to any number of factors. Note that the vector $M^F = M = (M_1....M_n)$ is the pre-union net import vector and is fixed throughout the analysis. This problem simply recasts the Kemp–Wan (1976) problem in welfare-maximization terms. We can normalize the pre-union foreign prices of all goods to unity. It is important to note that we are not assuming a fixed foreign-price vector. Because, as in Kemp–Wan (1976), we freeze the net import vector at the pre-union level, trade at the same foreign prices will obtain after the CU is formed and the welfare of the rest of the world is not reduced. Equation (6) is the trade-balance condition; (7) and (8) are the resource constraints; and (9) fixes imports at the pre-union level.

To solve this problem, we now form the following Lagrangean:

$$L = U - \left( \sum_i \lambda_i \left( C_i - \left[ \sum_j X_i^j (L_i^j, K_i^j) \right] + M_i \right) \right)$$
$$- \left( \sum_j \omega_j \left[ \sum_i L_i^j - L^j \right] \right) - \left( \sum_j \rho_j \left[ \sum_i K_i^j - K^j \right] \right)$$
$$- \left( \sum_i \eta_i \left( M_i - M_i^F \right) \right)$$

Maximization of the Lagrangean subject to the stated technology, resource, and import constraints yields the necessary conditions for a constrained optimum, as follows:

$$U_i = \lambda_i \ \forall i \tag{10}$$

$$\lambda_i = \eta_i \ \forall i \tag{11}$$

$$\lambda_i X_{i1}^j = \omega_j \quad or \quad L_i^j = 0 \forall i, j \tag{12}$$

$$\lambda_i X_{i2}^j = \rho_j \quad or \quad K_i^j = 0 \forall i, j \tag{13}$$

Equation (10), along with (12) and (13), implies that, for an interior solution, the marginal rate of substitution between any two goods, say good 1 and good 2, in consumption as well as production is the same value, $\frac{\lambda_1}{\lambda_2}$. Also, from (12), we know that $\lambda_i > 0, \forall i$. We could conveniently choose $\lambda_1 = 1$. Finally, from (11), we then know that

$$1 = \eta_1 \tag{14}$$

implying that

$$\lambda_i / \lambda_1 = \eta_i \ \forall i \tag{15}$$

That is, that the marginal rate of substitution in consumption as well as production is different from the foreign-price ratio. For instance, the marginal rate of substitution in consumption as well as production between goods $i$ and 1 is $\lambda_i / \lambda_1 = i$, whereas the foreign-price ratio is simply 1 (by construction). This implies a tariff imposed against the rest of the world on imports of good $i$. Note that, at an optimum, all other first-order conditions are to be met. In other words, given the import constraint, the second-best optimum is obtained by the use of suitable tariffs on imports from the rest of the world and with all other Paretian conditions being met. Because the optimal way to achieve the net import vector $M^F$ is as described previously, we can conclude that any other way of achieving $M^F$ can be (weakly) improved upon. Because $M^F$ was actually achieved pre-union, the pre-union situation can be (weakly) improved upon by the removal of all intra-union tariffs and by the use of a common external tariff (as was implied by the solution to the maximization problem). This is simply the Kemp–Wan (1976) result.

Now take a non-economic production objective into account. Thus, for instance, assume that each country $j$ within the CU wants the level of its production of good $i$ to be maintained at the pre-union level. This would imply additional constraints in the maximization exercise of the type

$$X_i^j = \bar{X}_i^j \; \forall j \qquad (16)$$

where $\bar{X}_i^j$ is the pre-union level of production of good $i$ in country $j$. The inclusion of this additional constraint alters the first-order conditions corresponding to $L_{ji}$ and $K_{ji}$. The new first-order conditions are

$$(\lambda_i + \delta) X_{i1}^j = \omega_j \, \forall \, j \tag{17}$$

and

$$(\lambda_i + \delta) X_{i2}^j = \rho_j \, \forall \, j \tag{18}$$

where $\delta$ is the multiplier attached to the new output objective. From (17) and (18), the marginal rates of substitution in production between good $i$ and all the other goods are different from the corresponding marginal rates of substitution in consumption between good $i$ and the other goods, implying that a production tax-cum-subsidy policy in each country is optimal. Also from (17) and (18), the marginal rate of substitution between L and K is the same in the production of the good $i$ as it is in the production of all other goods. Thus, there is no factor subsidy involved (except in the trivial sense of an equiproportionate subsidy on L and K used in the production of good $i$ – which, after all, is equivalent to a production subsidy on good $i$). Importantly, all other Paretian conditions should still be met for a constrained optimum, implying that the intra-union tariffs should be kept at zero. Any other way of achieving $X_i^j = \bar{X}_i^j$ can be (weakly) improved upon. Because $X_i^j = \bar{X}_i^j$ was actually achieved pre-union, the pre-union situation can be (weakly) improved upon and a (weakly) Pareto-superior outcome can be achieved.

Equally, it follows that the feasible welfare level of this CU would be even greater if the constraint $X_i^j = \bar{X}_i^j$ was weakened and rewritten as $\sum_j X_i^j = \sum_j \bar{X}_i^j$ so that the constraint is only an aggregate union-wide constraint (as discussed originally in Cooper and Massell [1965]). This result can also be readily extended to other "non-economic" constraints. A welfare-enhancing CU that does not harm or benefit non-members can be formed even if each member requires, for instance, that its manufacturing employment not fall. The supporting policy complementing the common external tariff will then be an employment-tax-cum subsidy (exactly as in Bhagwati and Srinivasan [1969]).

## 3.2 Free Trade Areas

It should be straightforward to see that a demonstration regarding welfare-improving FTAs is substantially more complex than that for CUs: In the case of an FTA, member-specific tariff vectors imply that the domestic-price vectors differ across member countries and the FTA generally fails to equalize marginal rates of substitution across its members.

This implies (in turn) that it is not possible to extend the *original* Kemp–Wan methodology to directly cover FTAs.

## 3.2.1 Partial Equilibrium Analysis

We consider first the simplest model capable of capturing the difference between the Kemp–Vanek–Ohyama–Wan CU and our FTA construction. Call the potential CU members Home and Foreign and the rest of the world ROW. Unless otherwise noted, lower-case letters are used to denote variables associated with Home and upper-case letters for those associated with Foreign. Assume that preferences are quasi-linear with the marginal utility of consumption of the numeraire good being constant. Also assume that the numeraire good uses only labor, whereas non-numeraire goods use labor and a sector-specific factor. These assumptions validate the partial-equilibrium analysis on which we rely in this chapter. Because we will be holding the prices in ROW constant by freezing the quantities traded by it, we define units of goods in such a manner that the prices in ROW are all unity.

In Figure 3.1, we depict the demands by Home and Foreign by dd and DD, respectively, for a non-numeraire good that is not produced at home. Home levies a tariff at rate $t^o$ and Foreign at rate $T^o > t^o$. Because the price in ROW is 1,

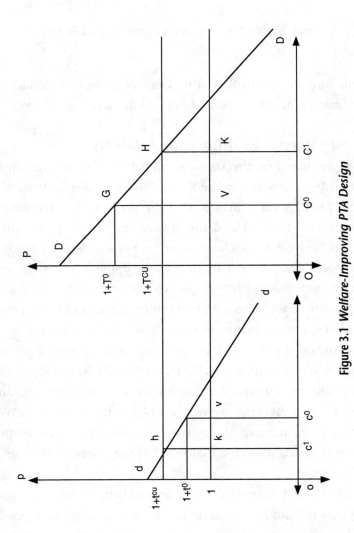

Figure 3.1 Welfare-Improving PTA Design

the domestic price in Home settles at $1 + t^o$ and in Foreign at $1 + T^o$. Home and Foreign consume and import quantities $oc^o$ and $OC^o$, respectively.

Suppose now that Home and Foreign form a CU, holding their joint imports at $oc^o + OC^o$. This would require setting the common external tariff at rate $t^{cu}(= T^{CU})$, where $T^o > t^{cu} > t^o$ and the joint demand by the member countries at price $1 + t^{cu}$ is $oc^1 + OC^1(= oc^o + OC^o)$. The increase in the price in Home lowers its welfare, whereas the decrease in price in Foreign does the opposite. However, because the marginal benefit of consumption is higher in Foreign in the initial equilibrium, the shift in consumption from Home to Foreign until the marginal benefits are equalized across members leads to a net gain for the CU as a whole. Thus, the CU improves the welfare of the CU and does not hurt the outside world. The loss to Home is measured by trapezium ghkv and the gain to Foreign by GHKV. But, because $kv = KV$ and $hk = HK$, the gain is necessarily bigger than the loss. Moreover, holding the union-wide imports fixed, the CU cannot improve on this equilibrium.

Suppose next that Home and Foreign form an FTA rather than the CU, each fixing the external tariff such that its imports are unchanged. Because the member countries do not produce the good, the only way to achieve this outcome is to fix the external tariffs at the initial rate and adopt the rules of origin (ROOs) whereby goods are not allowed to be trans-shipped; that is, goods consumed in Foreign are not permitted to be imported via Home at the lower tariff. Because there is no production of the good within the CU to take advantage of duty-free movement of goods produced inside the CU, under this arrangement, the outcome is the same as under the nondiscriminatory tariff. The FTA neither improves nor lowers welfare. Note that in this FTA equilibrium, prices (of the imported good) are different in the two partner countries – thereby creating the incentive to import the good through the low-tariff country and simply trans-ship it to the partner country by exploiting the free access to the latter's market. To prevent this type of trans-shipment (which effectively undermines the effort to maintain different tariff rates across the two partner countries), additional rules prohibiting such trans-shipment need to be introduced. These are the ROOs. We proceed by simply assuming that ROOs that effectively prevent trans-shipment of this type are in place and deferring a full discussion of what form these ROOs must take until later.

Let us now modify this simple case to allow for internal production. This is shown in Figure 3.2, where ss and SS represent the supply curves in Home and Foreign,

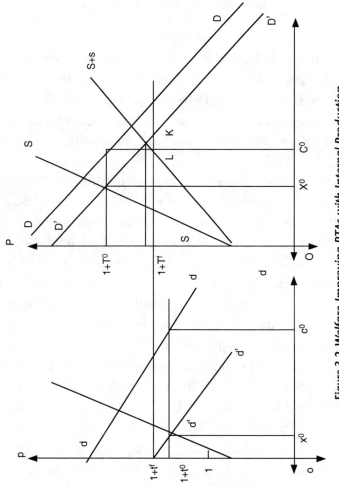

**Figure 3.2 Welfare-Improving PTAs with Internal Production**

respectively. As before, initially, each country levies a non-discriminatory tariff so that internal prices are given by $1 + t^o$ in Home and $1 + T^o$ in Foreign. At $1 + t^o$, the quantities consumed, produced, and imported equal $ox^o$, $oc^o$, and $x^o c^o$ in Home. The corresponding quantities in Foreign are $OX^o$, $OC^o$, and $X^o C^o$.

Suppose now that Home and Foreign form a CU, holding their joint imports fixed at $x^o c^o + X^o C^o$. This is accomplished by a common external tariff that lies between $t^o$ and $T^o$. Without demonstrating in Figure 3.2, we note that – as before – taking the total union-wide imports as fixed, the common external tariff maximizes the joint welfare of the CU by equating the marginal benefit and marginal cost of production with each other and across Home and Foreign.

Next, consider the formation of an FTA between Home and Foreign. This requires fixing the imports of each country at their pre-FTA level. To show how this works, subtract Home's initial imports, $x^o c^o$, from its demand curve and obtain dd as the residual demand that must be satisfied by within-union sources of supply. Analogously, obtain DD by subtracting $X^o C^o$ from DD as the demand in Foreign that must be satisfied by within-union sources of supply.

The key point to emphasize is that if imports are subject to different tariff rates and the ROOs forbid the low-tariff member from importing goods from outside for duty-free sales in the high-tariff country, the prices consumers pay in the two countries will differ from each other. In particular, they will be higher in the member with the higher tariff. Suppose, as will be shown to be true in the example, the post-FTA tariff that supports the pre-FTA imports is higher in Foreign than Home. It follows that all within-union output will be sold in Foreign. Conversely, if the post-FTA tariff happens to be higher in Home, all within-union output will be sold in that country. Only if the post-union tariff happens to be the same in the two countries – implying a coincidence of the FTA and CU solutions in the good under consideration – will the internal supply be sold in both countries.

In Figure 3.2, given the post-FTA tariff and hence that the consumer price is higher in Foreign, no within-union output is sold in Home. This means that the tariff in Home must be set at $t^f$ such that $1 + t^f$ represents the "reservation price." At this price, all demand in Home is satisfied by imports while its entire supply is sold in Foreign.

In Foreign, the available internal supply is the horizontal sum of $ss$ and $SS$ and is shown by the dotted line denoted $s + S$. To clear the market, the internal price must be $1 + T^f$, the height of the point of intersection of $DD$ and $s + S$. Thus, we have $T^f$ as the tariff in Foreign under the FTA. The reader can verify that the joint welfare of the CU members, as measured by the sum of their consumers' and producers' surpluses and tariff revenues, is higher at the FTA equilibrium than at the initial equilibrium.

The outcome in Figure 3.2 shows that the tariff rates that support country-specific pre-FTA imports in Home and Foreign are strictly different. This feature results from the fact that even after the entire within-union supply is diverted to Foreign, at $1 + t^f$, it falls short of the demand for within-union output. If within-union supply is sufficiently large to rule this out, *ex post*, the outcome will coincide with the CU outcome.

For example, suppose we shift ss horizontally to the right and SS horizontally to the left, holding the initial tariff rates and total union-wide supply at each price constant. This will shift dd to the right and DD to the left. Eventually, the horizontal line from $1 + t^f$ will come to pass through the intersection of $s + S$ and DD. At this configuration of demands, supplies, and initial tariffs, the FTA solution will just coincide with the CU solution in the good under consideration. As we continue to rotate ss clockwise and SS counterclockwise, the CU solution will continue to obtain with the internal supply sold in both CU members.

In Figure 3.2, holding the initial tariff rates and demands constant, if we rotate ss counterclockwise and SS clockwise, dd shifts to the left and DD to the right. In this case, $t^f$ and $T^f$ move in opposite directions. Thus, *ceteris paribus*, the lower the tariff in the country with smaller supply, the more likely that the outcome will be a strict FTA. And, conversely, the higher the tariff in the country with lower supply, the more likely that the outcome will coincide with the CU.

We conclude by noting a key point that will be important for proving our general result in the next subsection. For some products, the FTA solution may coincide with the CU solution. When it does not, a single producer price nevertheless rules within the CU, and it equals the consumer price in the member country with the higher tariff.

## 3.2.2 Proof in the General Case

To begin, we consider economies with only final goods. Intermediate inputs are added to the model in the next subsection. The proof in this case turns out to be surprisingly simple. The maintained assumption throughout is that in the event of differences in final prices between FTA partners on external imports, ROOs that effectively prevent transshipment of goods from low-tariff to high-tariff countries are in place. We defer our discussion of what form these ROOs may take until later.

We continue to denote Home variables by lower-case letters and Foreign variables by upper-case letters. Occasionally, we need to use the price vector in the ROW. We denote it by an upper-case letter with subscript W. A superscript 0 is used to identify the values of the variables in the initial pre-FTA equilibrium and a superscript f in the post-FTA equilibrium. If the pre- and post-FTA values of a variable happen to coincide, we use superscript 0.

The expenditure and revenue functions in Home and Foreign are again denoted as e(.) and E(.) and r(.) and R(.), respectively. The consumer price vectors are denoted $p$ and $P$ and welfare levels $u$ and $U$. We assume that the utility of Foreign in the post-FTA equilibrium is held fixed at its pre-FTA level through a lump-sum transfer from Home. The transfer may turn out to be positive or negative. Under this assumption, weak superiority of the FTA is established, provided

$$e(p^f, u^f) \geq e(p^f, u^o) \tag{19}$$

The income-expenditure inequality for the CU as a whole in the post-FTA equilibrium implies

$$e(p^f, u^f) + E(P^f, U^f)$$
$$= r(q^f) + R(q^f) + (p^f - P_W^o) m^o + (P^f - P_W^o) M^o \quad (20)$$

where $m^o$ and $M^o$ are vectors of quantities imported by Home and Foreign, respectively, from the ROW (i.e., not including the imports from each other) in the post-FTA equilibrium, which are the same as in the pre-FTA equilibrium. (Recall that, in the post-FTA equilibrium, we are fixing each country's import vector from the ROW at its pre-FTA level.) We note that $m^o$ is defined to include any goods that may have entered Home through Foreign in the pre-FTA equilibrium. That is, in fixing the external import vector of a member, we include in it any goods that may have imported or exported indirectly through the partner. A similar statement applies to $M^o$. Vector $P_W^o$ is the world price vector in the post-FTA equilibrium, which coincides with the pre-FTA equilibrium because we freeze the external trade vectors of both Home and Foreign at their pre-FTA levels. Vector qf is the producer-price vector in the post-FTA equilibrium, which is the same in Home and Foreign.

Recall that the essential difference between CUs and FTAs relates to the non-equalization of prices within the FTA. Also note that this non-equalization of prices inside the FTA applies only to consumer prices. Producer prices are equalized because producers of goods within the FTA are free to sell goods in either country. Using the subscript $c$ to denote consumers, we let $p_c^f$ and $P_c^f$ denote consumer prices in the home and the partner country and continue to let $p^f$ and $P^f$ denote producer prices in the home and the partner country. Goods can now be divided into three sets, denoted as $\alpha$, $\beta$, and $\gamma$. In set $\alpha$, we place goods for which the consumer price in the home country exceeds that in the partner ($p_c^f > P_c^f$). For these goods, all within-FTA output is sold in the home country so that the FTA-wide producer price coincides with the consumer price at home (so that $p^f = P^f = p_c^f$). In set $\beta$, we include goods for which the consumer price in the partner exceeds that in home ($p_c^f < P_c^f$). In this case, the FTA-wide producer price coincides with the consumer price in the partner (so that $p^f = P^f = P_c^f$). Finally, in set $\gamma$, we have goods for which consumer and producer prices coincide FTA-wide (i.e., $p^f = P^f = p_c^f = P_c^f$).

As noted previously, the Panagariya–Krishna FTA freezes the external-trade vector of the FTA members country by country. Free internal trade is assumed. Focusing on a world with just final goods and following exactly the same logic as that used to arrive at equation (4) for CUs, it is easy to show that the joint welfare of the FTA members is higher in the

FTA equilibrium if

$$p^f x^o + P^f X^o \geq p_c^f x^o + P_c^f X^o + \left(p_c^f - P_c^f\right) n^o \quad (21)$$

From the classification of goods into $\alpha$, $\beta$, and $\gamma$ goods and the previous discussion, we know that $p^f = P^f = p_c^f$ for all $\alpha$ goods, $p^f = P^f = P_c^f$ for all $\beta$ goods, and $p^f = P^f = P_c^f = p_c^f$ for all $\gamma$ goods. This, in turn, implies that for (21) to be satisfied, we need that

$$\left[\left(p_c^f - P_c^f\right)(X^o + N^o)\right]_\alpha + \left[\left(P_c^f - p_c^f\right)(x^o + n^o)\right]_\beta \geq 0 \quad (22)$$

From the earlier discussion regarding prices and the fact that domestic output in each member country is at least as large as its exports to its partner, it should be clear that all the terms in parentheses are greater than (or equal to) zero. The member countries in the FTA have (weakly) greater welfare than before; the rest of the world is no worse off than before. Thus, the FTA is necessarily welfare-improving overall. This completes the proof. An FTA designed along the lines of the Kemp–Wan CU is, indeed, necessarily welfare-improving (weakly) for the member countries and does not lower the welfare of the rest of the world.

### 3.2.3 Intermediate Inputs

This proof is extended readily to incorporate intermediate inputs. The first few steps should be sufficient to see how the extension works. Because intermediate inputs do not enter the utility function and, hence, the expenditure function, holding the utility of Foreign fixed through a lump-sum transfer at the pre-FTA level, Condition (19) continues to be necessary and sufficient for the FTA to weakly improve the joint welfare of the CU.

The main new issue that the presence of intermediate inputs raises is that of the ROOs. We impose the same rules of origin as in the previous subsection: both the final and intermediate inputs can move free of duty within the CU, provided they are produced internally. In the case of final goods, it does not matter whether the inputs used in it are imported or produced internally. As detailed in Chapter 5, irrespective of the proportion of internal value added, they must receive the duty-free treatment if the final stage of production takes place within the CU.

The buyers as well as sellers of intermediate inputs are firms. For reasons similar to those discussed in the previous subsection, the buyer prices can differ between the CU members, whereas the seller or producer price is the same. We now use a subscript I to distinguish inputs from outputs.

Thus, we denote by $p_I$ the vector of buyer prices and $q_I$ the vector of seller prices of inputs in Home. We can then write the revenue function, representing the maximized value of output of final and intermediate inputs, net of inputs used up, as $r(q, p_I, q_I)$. The partial derivatives of r(.) with respect to buyer prices of inputs, $p_I$, give the negative of the demand for inputs, and those with respect to seller prices, $q_I$, give the supplies of the inputs in Home. As before, partial derivatives of r(.) with respect to q give the outputs of final goods. Analogous notation applies to Foreign with upper-case letters replacing the lower-case letters everywhere, but with subscript I remaining unchanged. We can now replace equation (20) by

$$
\begin{aligned}
e\big(p^f, u^f\big) &+ E\big(P^f, U^f\big) \\
&= r\big(q^f, p_I^f, q_I^f\big) + R\big(q^f, P_I^f, q_I^f\big) \\
&\quad + \big(p^f - P_W^o\big)m^o + \big(P^f - P_W^o\big)M^o + \big(p_I^f - P_{IW}^o\big)m_I^o \\
&\quad + \big(P_I^f - P_{IW}^o\big)M_I^o
\end{aligned}
$$

where $P_{IW}^o$ denotes the vector of input prices in the ROW and $m_I^o$ and $M_I^o$ the vectors of inputs imported by Home and Foreign, respectively, from it. Note that the balance-of-trade condition of the ROW is now represented by $P_W^o(m_0 + M_o) + P_{IW}^o(m_I^o + M_I^o) = 0$. Note also that the revenue function for

Home is $r(q, p_I, q_I) = max.q.x + q_I.x_I - p_I.d_I$, where $x_I$ is the output vector and $d_I$ the demand vector of inputs in Home and that an analogous relationship holds for Foreign. These relationships, as well as the fact that the total input demand in, say, Home must be satisfied by domestic output, imports from the partner, or imports from the ROW (i.e., that $d_I^o = x_I^o + n_I^o + m_I^o$, where $n_I^o$ is the vector of inputs imported by Home from Foreign), gives us

$$\left[q^f x^o + q^f X^o\right] + \left[q_I^f x_I^o + q_I^f X_I^o\right]$$
$$\geq \left[p^f x^o + P^f X^o\right] + \left[p_I^f x_I^o + P_I^f X_I^o\right]$$
$$+ (p^f - P^f)n^o + \left(p_I^f - P_I^f\right)n_I^o \qquad (23)$$

which is similar to (21) and is proved to be true using identical logic as before.

### 3.2.4 Rules of Origin Necessary to Prevent Trans-Shipment

In proving the existence of welfare-improving FTAs, we have assumed so far that we use ROOs to prevent trans-shipment of imports. This implies that goods imported by the low-tariff member are not permitted to cross over to the high-tariff member country duty-free unless they have undergone some transformation. Thus, duty-free access necessarily applies to goods produced wholly within the

CU. Additionally, the goods containing foreign intermediate components are given duty-free status, provided the intermediates have undergone some transformation. Imported goods, whether intermediate or final, may not be transshipped in their original form.

In and of itself, this requirement may be seen as being somewhat incomplete for the following reason: In the FTA equilibrium that obtains, consumer prices differ across member countries (or else the FTA is, in fact, just a CU). Given the differing consumer prices across countries, agents have the incentive to import a given product through the low-tariff country, repackage and, thus, transform it into a trivially different good, availing themselves of the duty-free status in the higher-tariff partner country. This unrestrained transshipment would render the FTA arbitrarily close to a CU.

To avoid this possibility, we need to elaborate on the ROO necessary to support the FTA, keeping in mind that the proposed rule does not interfere with the equilibrium outcomes for welfare improvement described previously. We first describe the precise ROO required within our theoretical model and then discuss its practical counterpart.

**Rule of Origin.** A good wholly produced within the CU is given duty-free access to all countries within the CU.

Alternatively, if the good contains imported intermediates, it is allowed duty-free access, provided it differs from any of the intermediates it contains and is a good that existed prior to the formation of the FTA. Thus, it is also required that any new good (i.e., goods not existing in the pre-FTA equilibrium) be given duty-free access to CU countries only if it is wholly produced within the CU.

To explain how this ROO works (without interfering with the welfare-improving equilibrium outcome described in the proof), suppose there are 100 final and intermediate products in the pre-FTA equilibrium, which are denoted 1, 2, . . . , 100. Now consider a product crossing the intra-union border. The importer must first declare whether the product corresponds to one of these 100 products. If yes, the importer identifies the classification number of the product – for example, 80 – and the classification number of components imported from outside the CU. If these are all different from 80, the product enters duty-free. If one or more of them coincide with 80, duty-free status is not given.

Such an ROO, then, takes away the incentive for the importer to repackage 80 as a different product. If declared as a new product different from product 80, duty-free status is denied. If declared as product 80, that the components coincide with the product breaches the transformation rule, and duty-free status is again denied.

Thus, our rule ensures that there is no trans-shipment of imports from the low-tariff member to the high-tariff member without imposing any new constraints on the problem. It is important to note that the rule prohibiting the trans-shipment of products (product 80 in the example) does not imply a more restrictive environment than in the pre-FTA equilibrium. Any trans-shipment that existed in the pre-FTA equilibrium continues to reach the country of its final destination; only they now come directly to that country because the external-trade vector of each member includes not only the imports it received directly from the rest of the world, but also those it receives through the partner in the form of trans-shipments. Therefore, the ROO fully preserves the proof.

Thus, it has been shown that there exists a (theoretical) ROO capable of supporting the FTA equilibrium identified. We can now ask how this rule can be applied in practice. For most products, the transformation rule can be applied using the harmonized system of classification. Duty-free status is necessarily given to a product that is produced wholly within the CU or belongs to a classification category different from all components imported from extra-union trading partners. The harmonized system of classification, which is used by virtually all countries, disaggregates products up to the ten-digit level. In most cases, this level of disaggregation suffices to distinguish products that satisfy our theoretical rule from those that have been simply repackaged and do not satisfy it. For example, an automobile imported from an outside country and simply repackaged will fail this test because it will fail to move from one classification category to another.

The transformation requirement stated herein and its implementation is entirely consistent with the ROOs implemented in actual practice — in NAFTA, for instance. Appendix 3.1 reproduces a description of the NAFTA ROOs from LaNasa (1993). It should be readily evident that the first three rules described there closely match this transformation rule. Moreover, to rule out trivial transformations of the type considered previously in this subsection, NAFTA ROOs explicitly state that "mere dilution with water or another substance that do not materially alter the characteristics of the product do not count as a transformation."

The member countries in the FTA just constructed each have individual tariff vectors, with the tariff vector defined as the difference between the world price $P_W^o$ and the consumer-price vector within each country. The theory, therefore, provides specific guidance as to what form the external-tariff vector in a (welfare-improving) FTA or a CU ought to take (i.e., it should deliver the same level of trade with the rest of the world as initially, thereby eliminating trade diversion). However, there remain interesting practical problems with regard to the choice of this external-tariff vector, the elimination of internal barriers, and the setting of appropriate ROOs in the CU. It is to these issues that we turn next.

## 3.3 Implementation

The preceding discussion of necessarily welfare-improving CUs and FTAs provided a precise description of the tariff vectors that ought to be implemented in these agreements. Specifically, internal barriers are to be completely eliminated and the external-tariff vector in both cases (i.e., the CU or the FTA) should eliminate trade diversion — member countries should continue to import the same amounts from the rest of the world as they did initially.[9] Can these

---

[9] It should, of course, be clear by now that with the Kemp–Wan CU, the trade vector of the member countries is restricted to be the same as initially for the CU members as a whole. With FTAs, this constraint needs to be met separately for each member country.

tariffs be implemented in practice? And where do existing GATT/WTO provisions stand in relation to the theoretical specification?

Article XXIV of the GATT (see Appendix 2.1), which permits the formation of PTAs, also originally stipulated *broadly* that internal preferences needed to be complete (i.e., that internal barriers between the members were to be completely eliminated) and that external trade barriers were not to be more restrictive than initially. As discussed herein, a number of questions arose in connection with GATT regulations regarding both internal and external tariffs: some related to their economic merit, others to implementation and possible abuse given the ambiguous and imprecise wording adopted in the original text of the GATT. As will be discussed further, although the more recent "Understanding on the Interpretation" of Article XXIV issued by the GATT in 1994 clarified some of these issues, other questions still remain.

### 3.3.1  Barriers to Trade with Non-Members

On external tariffs, the original GATT requirement was that external barriers not be more restrictive than initially. For FTAs, because countries retain individual tariff vectors, this could be taken to imply that no tariff was to rise. For CUs, because a *common* external tariff was to be chosen and initial tariffs on the same good likely varied across countries, the tariff vector would necessarily change for each country. The expectation then was that the "general incidence" of trade barriers would not be higher or more restrictive than before. Given the imprecise phrasing, there was once more substantial ambiguity as to what is implied: Should the common external tariff equal the unweighted mean of initial tariffs in the member countries? Should it be the trade-weighted mean? Or something else?

As Dam (1970), Bhagwati (1993), and several others have noted, it is clear that Article XXIV's ambiguity in this regard left ample room for opportunistic (i.e., protectionist) behavior by member countries against non-members. The 1994 "Understanding on the Interpretation" of Article XXIV issued by the GATT (see Appendix 2.1) provided substantial clarity on the issue of measurement and choice of the common external tariff — indicating that the GATT secretariat would compute weighted average tariff rates and duties collected in accordance with the methodology used in the assessment of tariff offers in the Uruguay Round of trade negotiations and examine trade flow and other data to arrive at suitable measures of non-tariff barriers. Although this relieves, at least partially, the issue of measurement of external barriers and the comparison with barriers in place initially, the economic concern regarding trade diversion is not addressed. Clearly, leaving external barriers at their initial level and removing internal barriers does not eliminate trade diversion (as theoretically required in the Kemp–Wan and Panagariya–Krishna constructions of welfare-improving PTAs). Indeed, with this configuration, trade diversion is practically guaranteed.

Choosing or designing tariff vectors ex-ante that would ensure zero trade diversion, good by good, is hardly more promising, for the exact sensitivities of external trade flows to external barriers of the CU or FTA are difficult or impossible to estimate accurately. So, there is little prospect of identifying the exact trade-diversion–eliminating Kemp–Wan tariff vector and implementing it in practice.[10] Nevertheless, designing other disciplines to minimize diversion is less difficult; one can certainly say that simultaneously lowering external barriers with the formation of a CU or

---

[10] See, however, the paper by Srinivasan (1997), which attempts to identify and characterize the Kemp–Wan tariff vector in the context of a particular economic model.

an FTA is likely to lower the degree of trade diversion (by minimizing the substitution away from the goods supplied by the rest of the world to within-union goods). McMillan (1993) suggested as a test of admissibility of any PTA the measurement (estimation) of whether that PTA will result in less trade with the rest of the world.[11] In a similar spirit, Bhagwati (1993) suggested that the requirement of a simultaneous *pro rata* reduction of external trade barriers with the progressive elimination of internal barriers could replace the current requirements.

## 3.3.2  Internal Barriers to Trade

On internal barriers to trade, two questions arise. The first relates to coverage: Do GATT regulations require a removal of *all* internal barriers? The second relates to timing: How much time do countries have to comply with the rules? On the former issue, it should be clarified that whereas the putative intent of the GATT was to require that internal barriers be eliminated completely, the actual text of the GATT only required that restrictions be eliminated on "substantially all

---

[11] Of course, the Kemp–Wan and Panagariya–Krishna schemes both require that the PTA trade *exactly* the same amount as before. A PTA that trades no less, as in the McMillan test, is not necessarily welfare-improving, as Winters (1997) argued.

trade." The ambiguous phrasing through the use of the qualifier "substantially" opened up a number of possibilities for abuse. Whether "substantial" should have be taken to imply a full 100 percent or something smaller was not clear and has not yet been clarified. In this context, for a given level of external tariffs, member-country welfare is not necessarily maximized with zero internal barriers.[12] From a purely economic standpoint, given the level of external tariffs, welfare may well be maximized by maintaining some *particular* level of internal restrictions. It may, therefore, be *potentially* argued that the ambiguous phrasing permitting non-elimination of internal barriers allowed member countries to aim at welfare-maximizing outcomes; this is, however, quite unlikely. Any retention of internal barriers within PTAs is probably better explained by selective protectionist motivations on the part of country governments. Separately, it may be imagined that non-member countries would have an incentive to monitor and ensure the full dismantling of

---

[12] It is important that the elimination of internal tariffs maximizes the welfare of member countries for a given level of external trade (as in Kemp–Wan) and not for a given level of the external tariffs. With fixed tariffs, member-country welfare may well be maximized with internal tariffs that are non-zero.

internal trade barriers within PTAs. However, it is also quite likely that the welfare of countries outside the CU is higher when the discrimination against them is lower (i.e., when internal preferences are less than complete). *Ex-post*, the external monitoring incentive is, therefore, minimal. On the question of the timing and phasing out of internal barriers to trade, GATT rules – rather than requiring an immediate removal of internal barriers in a PTA – allowed for this to take place within a "reasonable length of time," once again permitting substantial ambiguity in understanding and room for abuse.[13]

### 3.3.3 Rules of Origin

In FTAs, importers have a potential incentive to import goods into the bloc through the member country imposing the lowest tariff on that good and then to trans-ship that good into higher-tariff member countries by availing themselves of the duty-free treatment within the bloc. To prevent this circumvention of the independent tariffs

---

[13] The more recent "Understanding on the Interpretation" of Article XXIV issued in 1994 clarifies that the "reasonable length of time" should exceed ten years in only "exceptional cases."

desired by member countries, however, FTAs need to be supported by ROOs, which specify the circumstances under which a good may be given duty-free treatment within the CU.[14]

The discussion in the previous subsection provided a welfare-theoretic basis for simple ROOs: Goods that undergo any genuine value-added transformation within the CU must be allowed to move duty-free within the CU. For any good entirely produced outside the CU, trade-deflection is to be prevented by imposing effectively on both direct imports and any trans-shipped units the external tariff that is chosen by the member country where the good is eventually consumed. ROOs are more complex in practice, however: they are differently concerned (depending on the good) with the fractional content of the good that is required to be produced within the CU for the good to qualify for duty-free status.[15] More important, although the putative intention of ROOs is to simply prevent deflection of trade, it has

[14] Because, in practice, at least some traded goods are not covered by the common external barriers of a CU, ROOs are often used in CUs as well.

[15] See the papers by Estevadeordal and Suominen (2003) and Krishna (2004) for a detailed discussion of the different ways in which ROOs are specified in practice.

been argued that these rules have been used more flexibly as instruments of commercial policy.

That the opportunity to set ROOs would be abused to achieve other ends should come as no surprise to anyone even moderately familiar with the political economy of trade-policy determination. Although we may hope for FTA rules to be designed by welfare-maximizing governments concerned with the enhancement of internal efficiency and equity toward non-members, in practice, the ROOs are determined in intensely political contexts in which a variety of additional factors influence policy. Governments are under great pressure to deviate from the high path of choosing ROOs to simply prevent trade deflection toward fixing rules that favor politically active and aggressive constituencies in the economy. Because in an FTA there are no internal tariffs and because external tariffs themselves cannot be raised to further disadvantage non-member countries, it has been argued that to please their constituencies and protect them from the economic changes that come about due to the entry into the FTA,[16] governments manipulate ROOs to protect

---

[16] Of course, the choice of entry into the FTA itself is subject to a political calculation. For models of endogenous bilateral agreements, see Chapter 5.

both domestic suppliers of final and intermediate goods. This may happen in the following ways.

1. Protection for final good suppliers
   Consider a final goods supplier in a member country facing greater competition from suppliers in other member countries due to the impending elimination of internal barriers of trade within the FTA. Consider further that this foreign competition uses intermediates in its production from outside the FTA. Due to the political pressures brought to bear on the domestic government – whether it is from capitalists, affected voters, or displaced workers – that government will have reasons to negotiate intra-union content criteria severe enough to push those competing goods out of the duty-free category. In so doing, they will insulate the home-country supplier from that greater competition but will also undermine the intended competitive enhancement from joining an FTA.
2. The creation of a captive market for within-union producers of intermediate goods
   Governments can negotiate for ROOs that specify a high degree of domestic (i.e., within-bloc) content, significantly diverting demand from goods produced with

foreign intermediates to goods produced using intermediates from within the FTA.

However, this use of ROOs undermines the two key rules imposed by the WTO on its members for FTA formation. Although complete internal liberalization is sought by the WTO, it is negated by the selective use of ROOs. Further, although the WTO requires that trade barriers against non-members not be raised by FTA members, the use of stringent ROOs would divert imports of intermediates away from non-member exporters, even if external tariffs are maintained at the same level as before.[17]

To what extent ROOs are used to prevent trade deflection and to what extent they are politically motivated commercial-policy instruments is ultimately an empirical question. Although empirical research in this area is still in its infancy, Cadot, Estevadeordal, and Suwa-Eisenmann (2003) recently provided some interesting results. They examine directly the possible use of ROOs to achieve protection

---

[17] Ironically, however, highly severe ROOs may result in greater imports from the rest of the world than before owing to the preference of importers to pay the external tariff rather than comply with demanding domestic-content standards.

for final goods producers and the creation of a captive market for intra-union suppliers of intermediate goods, as discussed previously. Using measures of ROO restrictiveness developed by Estevadeordal (2000), they measure the effects of ROOs on Mexican imports to the U.S. market, finding ROOs a large enough negative influence on intra-union trade flows to offset the tariff preferences granted by the trade agreement. Further, the creation of a protected market for intermediate goods producers also appears to be a key determinant of the ROOs chosen.

# Geography and Preferential Trade Agreements: The "Natural" Trading Partners Hypothesis

T he previous chapters discussed some reasons for why economists have been divided on the wisdom of PTAs. Following Viner's (1950) demonstration that the net-welfare effects of PTAs are unpredictable and possibly negative, many attempts were made to refine the theory and identify member-country characteristics that would ensure welfare improvement and, thus, the welfare ambiguities associated with preferential trade (e.g., see Meade [1955], Lipsey [1958, 1960], and Johnson [1962], and a later synthesis by McMillan and McCann [1980]). However, these efforts yielded results that did not have any greater direct operational significance than did Viner (1950). That is, they did not yield any direct insights on which country characteristics would make trade creation rather than trade diversion a likely outcome and, therefore, which particular countries would be more desirable as partners in a PTA.

More recently, increasing emphasis has been placed on geographic proximity as a criterion for membership in a PTA. Regionalism in preferential trade has been argued by some as being key to generating better economic outcomes. Thus, Wonnacott and Lutz (1987), Krugman (1991), and Summers (1991) each proposed geographical proximity as a key predictor of trade creation and welfare improvement in PTAs, calling proximate trading partners "natural" partners for a PTA. Thus, for instance, Wonnacott and Lutz (1987) state:

Trade creation is likely to be great, and trade diversion small, if the prospective members of an FTA are natural trading partners. Several points are relevant: Are the prospective members already major trading partners? If so, the FTA will be reinforcing. . . . Are the prospective members close geographically? [Preferential] groupings of distant nations may be inefficient. . . .

As Bhagwati (1993) notes, this argument that PTAs should have a regional orientation depends on a syllogism. The first premise is that geographically proximate countries have higher volumes of trade with each other than do more distant ones; the second premise is that trade blocs between countries that already trade disproportionately are less likely to divert trade. Thus, Krugman (1991) states:

> To reemphasize why this matters: If a disproportionate share of world trade would take place between trading blocs even in the absence of a preferential trading agreement, then gains from trade creation within blocs are likely to outweigh any possible losses from external trade diversion.

Figure 2.1 models the second premise. All of country A's trade is initially with country B. Preferential tariff liberalization with B brings welfare gains. Preferential tariff liberalization with the less significant trading partner, C, is more likely to be welfare-decreasing.[18] And then, because

---

[18] This policy prescription has been challenged by Panagariya (1997) and Bhagwati and Panagariya (1996). Armed with a series of examples generated by assuming, alternately, that the home country is large and small and that imports from the rest of the world and the partner country are homogeneous and differentiated, *inter alia*, they argue that trade theory offers no such general presumption. Preferential reduction in tariffs by one country vis-à-vis its significant trading partner, the country with which its volume of trade is larger, may in fact improve welfare less than a reduction in tariffs vis-à-vis its less significant trading partner, and a preferential reduction of tariffs by one country vis-à-vis its geographically proximate trading partner may improve welfare less than a reduction in tariffs vis-à-vis a geographically distant trading partner. Thus, they state

geographically proximate countries do trade (dis - proportionately) with each other – the first premise – many analysts have felt compelled to conclude that a PTA between geographically proximate countries is more likely to result in welfare improvement.

In addition to the academic interest in this idea deriving from theoretical arguments of the type discussed herein, the question of natural trading partners is immensely interesting for policy reasons. Many existing PTAs are, indeed, regional. In addition, many extensions of existing arrangements along regional lines, such as the expansion of the NAFTA to include Chile, Argentina, and other South American countries or that of the European Union (EU) to include countries from Eastern and Central Europe, are currently being debated and discussed in policy circles.

To what extent, then, is this argument a robust one? Is it true that the argument that trade creation is more likely with preferential tariff reductions against geographically proximate partners holds up when we consider more complex worlds (in terms of production and consumption structures)

that "[Thus], while volume of trade as a criterion for judging FTAs to be benign is to be rejected, we must also add that linking this to *regionalism* and thus declaring regional FTAs to be more benign than non-regional FTAs is additionally wrong."

than the one represented in Figure 2.1? It is with this question that this chapter is concerned. However, as already noted, theory offers few direct answers to this question; an empirical evaluation is necessary. Therefore, the present approach is to use a theoretical framework and econometric methodology that are tightly linked with each other so that the econometric estimates may be fed back into the theoretical framework (in particular, into the theoretical expressions concerning welfare change that we derive from the theory). Trade data from the United States are then used to arrive at welfare estimates with preferential tariff liberalization against a number of partner countries at different levels of geographic proximity to the United States. Examining the correlations between the welfare estimates and distance will help evaluate the natural trading partners theory.

There have already been a number of attempts to investigate econometrically the impact of specific PTAs. None, however, has addressed the questions that this research attempts to tackle. Further, as Srinivasan, Whalley, and Wooton (1993) point out in their comprehensive survey on measuring the effects of regionalism, a significant problem with these studies is that they usually lack microeconomic underpinnings, which makes the welfare analysis of even actual arrangements difficult and precludes entirely the possibility of welfare comparisons of alternate potential PTAs. In contrast, the framework presented here has the benefit that it easily permits welfare analysis and comparisons because, by design, it is firmly grounded in an optimization framework. Other merits (and demerits) of the methodology used here are discussed later in this chapter.

## 4.1 Modeling Preferential Trade Liberalization: Theory

In classic Vinerian fashion, we consider a trading world that is composed of three countries: country A; its prospective partner, country B; and a third country C, representing the rest of the world. Each country only produces a single good, some of which it exports to pay for its consumption (imports) of the other two goods.[19] Normalizing the border price of

---

[19] Thus, the analysis that follows is conducted under the traditional "Armington" (1969) assumption. For a critical discussion on the use of this assumption in analyzing the welfare effect of PTAs, particularly when the relevant cross-elasticities in consumption are restricted by assumption as well, see the superb discussion of Deardorff and Stern (1994). Because the present analysis will proceed to estimate these elasticities instead, the criticisms of Deardorff and Stern (1994) do not apply with the same force.

each good to be one,[20] country A's budget constraint can be expressed as

$$E(1, 1 + t_B, 1 + t_C, W) = R(1, 1 + t_B, 1 + t_C, V)$$
$$+ t_B M_B + t_C M_C \qquad (1)$$

where $E$ is the expenditure function associated with country A; $R$ is the revenue function; $W$ denotes country A's welfare; and $t_B$, $t_C$, $M_B$, and $M_C$ denote tariffs imposed against and imports from countries B and C, respectively. Starting from this initial situation, we are interested in analyzing the effect of a preferential reduction in tariffs imposed by country A against country B. To get to this, we totally differentiate (1) and let $E_i$ denote the partial derivatives of E with respect to the $i'^{\text{th}}$ domestic price to obtain

$$E_B dt_B + E_c dt_C + E_W dw = t_B d M_B + M_B dt_B$$
$$+ t_c d M_C + M_C dt_C \qquad (2)$$

[20] Thus, we make the small-country assumption and ignore terms of trade effects. The theoretical analysis can, of course, be readily extended to allow for terms of trade changes. However, as we report and discuss shortly, our analysis of the data implies that we are unable to reject the null that terms-of-trade effects are non-existent. Thus, we chose to drop the terms of trade rather than carry them along in this chapter. For a theoretical treatment with terms-of-trade effects present, see Panagariya (1997).

Because the partials of the expenditure function, $E_i$, denote consumption of the $i'^{\text{th}}$ good, it follows that

$$E_B = M_B \quad \text{and that}$$
$$E_C = M_C$$

(2) therefore reduces to

$$E_W dW = t_B dM_B + t_C dM_C \tag{3}$$

where $E_W > 0$ because it is simply the inverse of the marginal utility of income (which helps convert the real-income changes on the righthand side into welfare units). Expression (3) has the familiar intuitive interpretation: For welfare improvement to be guaranteed, both imports from the partner country and the rest of the world should increase. If, alternately, imports from the partner country increase, $dM_B > 0$, implying trade creation, but imports from the rest of the world decrease, $dM_C < 0$, implying classic trade diversion, welfare might drop instead.[21]

To relate this expression to country characteristics, we make use of the fact that the compensated import-demand

---

[21] Another interpretation of (3) is that welfare will increase if a policy change results in increased tariff revenue at the initial tariff levels.

functions, $M_B$ and $M_C$, themselves are a function of prices and welfare. Thus, they can be expressed as

$$M_B = M_B(1, 1 + t_B, 1 + t_C, W) \qquad (4)$$

and

$$M_C = M_C(1, 1 + t_B, 1 + t_C, W) \qquad (5)$$

Totally differentiating (4) and (5) gives us

$$dM_B = M_{BB}dt_B + M_{BC}dt_C + M_{BW}dW \qquad (6)$$

and

$$dM_C = M_{CB}dt_B + M_{CC}dt_C + M_{CW}dW \qquad (7)$$

Because we only consider a preferential tariff reduction with respect to B, we can set $dt_C = 0$. Then, substituting (6) and (7) into (3) gives us

$$(E_W - t_B M_{BW} - t_C M_{CW})dW = (t_B M_{BB} + t_C M_{CB})dt_B \qquad (8)$$

Because $E$ is homogeneous of degree one in prices, $E_W$ is also homogeneous of degree one in prices. Using Euler's theorem, we then have

$$E_W = E_{AW} + (1 + t_B)E_{BW} + (1 + t_C)E_{CW} \qquad (9)$$

Substituting (9) into (8) gives us a final expression for welfare similar to the one derived by McMillan and McCann (1980):

$$HdW = (t_B M_{BB} + t_C M_{CB})dt_B \qquad (10)$$

where

$$H = E_{AW} + E_{BW} + E_{CW} = \left(\frac{\partial(E_A + E_B + E_C)}{\partial I}\right) E_W \qquad (11)$$

and where, clearly, $H$ is positive, if all goods are normal in consumption, as will be assumed here.

Expression (10) tells us that welfare improvement is guaranteed if imports from the partner country are substitutes for home-country output and complementary to imports from the rest of the world.[22] Two observations may be made here. First, (3) indicates that the methodology followed in many previous analyses – of simply adding up the estimated volumes of trade created and diverted (i.e, changes in the volumes of trade with respect to the partner country and the rest of the world) – is somewhat incorrect. Second, given initial conditions, (11) implies that the term "H" is independent

[22] This is, of course, a sufficient condition and not a necessary one. If the trade creation term on the righthand side of (10) dominates the trade-diversion term, welfare will go up even if the rest of the world output and partner-country output are substitutes.

of the particular bilateral tariff reduction being considered. In other words, if we were to compare the welfare effect of a preferential reduction in tariffs by A against country B with the welfare effect when tariffs are preferentially reduced against C instead, a comparison of the righthand side of (10) in the two cases would suffice to establish a welfare ranking. Of course, to estimate the righthand side of (10) for preferential tariff reductions against each potential partner country, we need to estimate the own-price and cross-price effects on imports from the partner country and the rest of the world in each case. It is to this problem that we turn next.

## 4.2  Modeling Preferential Trade Liberalization: Econometrics

To estimate the own- and cross-price effects in (10), we use a version of the Rotterdam model[23] developed by Barten

---

[23] A popular alternative and closely related model, the "Almost Ideal Demand System" (AIDS) developed by Deaton and Muellbauer (1980a), has also been used to estimate trade elasticities. For innovative applications of this model to study integration issues, see Winters (1984, 1985). The crucial difference between this model and the Rotterdam framework is that the latter is an approximation to the solution of the first-order conditions for optimizing any arbitrary utility function, whereas the former is an

(1966) and Theil (1965) and used in estimating U.S. trade elasticities by Marquez (1994). The Rotterdam model embodies, by design, all the properties of utility maximization – it recognizes the interdependence between spending decisions and does not treat trade elasticities as autonomous parameters.[24] Individuals determine their spending on domestic and foreign goods by maximizing a utility function, $U(q_1 \ldots q_n)$, subject to a budget constraint, $\Sigma_j p_j q_j = I$,[25] where I denotes income and $j$ is a country index. Obtaining the first-order conditions for maximizing *any* $U(.)$ and totally differentiating the associated system of

exact solution to a specific utility function and is, therefore, derived from explicit demand functions. However, as Deaton and Muellbauer (1980a, p. 317) note, "For the prediction of demand, this difference is not vitally important." Our own preference for the Rotterdam framework is due to the generality of the underlying utility function and also because, in contrast to the AIDS, it *directly* delivers the parameters that are required for our welfare calculations.

[24] Marquez (1991) also compares trade elasticities estimated using the Rotterdam model with those obtained using conventional log-linear models to show that the differential between these two models is significant from both an economic and statistical point of view.

[25] The spending decisions here, in common with much of the previous literature, suffer from at least the limitations that they ignore intertemporal substitution and that labor supply and asset-holding decisions are taken to be separable from decisions to consume domestic and foreign products.

Marshallian demands, functions of income, and prices yields the following expression for the demand for the $i'^{\text{th}}$ product:

$$(\omega_{it})dlnq_{it} = \left[\frac{\partial(p_{it}q_{it})}{\partial I_t}\right] dln\left(\frac{I}{P}\right)_t$$
$$+ \Sigma_j \left[\left(\frac{p_{it}p_{jt}}{I_t}\right)\left(\frac{\partial h_{it}}{\partial p_{jt}}\right)\right] dlnp_{jt} \quad (12)$$

where

$$\omega_{it} = \left[\frac{(p_{it}q_{it})}{I_t}\right]$$

$p_{jt} = (1 + \tau_{jt})p_{xjt} = $ domestic price of good $j$

$dlnp_t = \Sigma_j (\omega_{jt})dlnp_{jt}$

$\tau_{jt}$ is the tariff rate on imports from $j$

and

$p_{xjt}$ is the border price of the $j^{\text{th}}$ good

To implement (12) empirically, the Rotterdam model restricts the marginal budget share

$$\mu_i = \left[\frac{\partial(p_{it}q_{it})}{\partial I_t}\right]$$

and the Slutsky coefficients

$$\pi_{ij} = \left(\frac{p_{it}p_{jt}}{I_t}\right)\left(\frac{\partial q_{it}}{\partial p_{jt}}\right)$$

to be invariant to changes in income and prices.[26] The marginal budget share measures the additional amount spent on the $i'^{th}$ good, when income increases by one dollar. The Slutsky coefficient measures the compensated price effect of a change in the price of the $j'^{th}$ good on purchases of the $i'^{th}$ good. Treating these parameters as autonomous transforms (12) into

$$(\omega_{it})dlnq_{it} = \mu_i dln\left(\frac{I}{P}\right)_t + \Sigma_j(\pi_{ij})dlnp_{jt} + r_{it} \quad (13)$$

where $r_{it}$ is a random disturbance containing the second-order approximation terms induced by the assumed

---

[26] As Marquez (1991) notes, some critics of the Rotterdam model have pointed out that treating $\mu$ and $\pi$ as invariant to income and prices implies Cobb–Douglas preferences. In response, the literature has pointed out that this criticism, known as the "McFadden critique," stems from not differentiating between macro and micro parameters. Indeed, Barnett (1979, 1981) derives implications for macro behavior assuming that individuals behave according to the Rotterdam model without treating the micro parameters as invariant to income and prices. Using several theorems on stochastic limits, he derives the Rotterdam model with constant parameters, where the second-order approximation error due to the discrepancy between the macro and micro parameters has an expected value of zero. See also Clements et al. (1996) for a more recent discussion and derivation. Overall, the McFadden critique is not very relevant for empirical work with aggregate data, as Deaton and Muellbauer (1980b, p. 77) note.

constancy of $\mu_i$ and $\pi_{ij}$.[27,28] Estimation of the demand system (13) gives us own- and cross-price effects (the relevant $\pi_{ij}$s) that may be substituted back into (10) to get estimates of welfare change due to preferential tariff reduction.

For the parameters of the Rotterdam model to be consistent with utility maximization, they need to satisfy the following restrictions:[29]

1. The adding up constraint on marginal budget shares:

$$\Sigma_j \mu_j = 1 \qquad (14)$$

---

[27] The income and price elasticities associated with (13) are $\frac{\mu_i}{\omega_{it}}$ and $\frac{\pi_{ij}}{\omega_{it}}$, respectively.

[28] Importantly, as Panagariya (1997) notes, assuming specific utility functions, like the Constant Elasticity of Substitution (CES), imposes strong restrictions on the relationship between the elasticities being estimated and expenditure shares. Although our formulation does not impose any particular functional form on the utility function, it is restrictive in assuming the marginal budget shares and the Slutsky coefficients to be constant. However, these do not, to our knowledge, bias the results in any specific direction.

[29] The work of Marquez (1994), using U.S. trade data, finds support in the data for these restrictions — as do we (see the discussion of results in Chapters 4 and 5). A discussion of earlier tests of these restrictions and the associated history is provided in Deaton and Muellbauer (1980b).

2. Homogeneity of demand:

$$\Sigma_j \pi_{ij} = 0 \forall i \qquad (15)$$

3. Symmetry:

$$\pi_{ij} = \pi_{ji} \ \forall \ i, j, \quad i \neq j \qquad (16)$$

The merits of the demand system outlined herein can be seen when contrasted with alternative demand systems that have commonly been used in the international trade literature: log-linear demand systems and the gravity framework.

As Marquez (1991) points out, most previous estimates of U.S. trade elasticities used log-linear models that assume that the trade elasticities themselves are autonomous parameters. Because an elasticity is the ratio between a marginal propensity and an expenditure share, and because expenditure shares vary through time (as can be easily verified for U.S. trade data), the assumed invariance of elasticities assumes that marginal propensities change to offset these changes in expenditure shares – an assumption with no theoretical basis.[30] An additional weakness of many previous

---

[30] Further, if individuals maximize utility subject to a linear budget constraint, the log-linear specification implies directly that the income elasticity and the own-price elasticity are one and that cross-price elasticities are zero – making their estimation redundant.

studies is that they often neglect the interdependence between spending decisions as well. Further, in estimating log-
linear demand systems (most commonly used in estimating
trade elasticities), it is, of course, commonly assumed that
the parameters being estimated – the elasticities – are constant. However, it is well known (e.g., see Coopmans and
Uzawa [1990]) that constancy of the elasticities taken together with the fact that the budget constraint is met with
equality implies that the own-price and cross-price elasticity
are already theoretically determined to be $-1$ and $0$, respectively. Because the parameters are then predetermined, their
estimation is redundant. Given that the estimation of own-
and cross-price effects is crucial in determining the welfare
effect in (10), it is not clear what a model that predetermines
these parameters is telling us.[31]

Using the gravity model in the current context poses yet
other difficulties. The work of Deardorff (1997), *inter alia*,
has shown that gravity equations specifying a relationship
between bilateral trade volume on the one hand and in-
comes and transport costs on the other can be quite easy to
derive. However, general versions of such gravity equations

---

[31] Much of this discussion of the log-linear model is borrowed directly
from Marquez (1991).

include a host of additional variables on the righthand side. In particular, supply prices of *all* trading partners, the corresponding tariffs applied by the home country, and transport costs that apply to *all* of these imports appear on the righthand side of *every* equation for bilateral trade. Empirical implementation of the gravity equation has usually not included these variables. Departures from the basic gravity specifications (which explain bilateral trade volumes, including only income levels for the country pair and the geographic distance between them) are represented only by a single PTA dummy variable. This is problematic for a variety of reasons. Importantly, the resulting estimation framework is not able to distinguish between the effects of bilateral terms of trade movements, of changes in bilateral trade barriers that come about as a result of MFN trade reductions, and of preferential changes in bilateral trade barriers. Bilateral trade prices are also not included on the righthand side. In a context in which the primary question is the impact of relative price changes on trade volume, this approach raises questions as to what the estimated trade-bloc coefficients (attached to the PTA dummies) are telling us.[32]

[32] Further, out of apparent necessity, the gravity-equation PTA dummy coefficients are estimated (e.g., in Frankel [1997]) under the assumption that they are common across all country pairs,

In these estimations, we consider a single "home country": the United States. For the United States, we consider twenty-four different partner countries. In estimating the demand system, one option is to estimate a full-blown multilateral demand system that would include (in the U.S. case) twenty-six equations (i.e., twenty-four partner countries, home country + rest of the world). However, this leaves a large number of parameters to estimate. In particular, when considering preferential tariff reductions against any one country, the cross-price term that would need to be included in (10) (to calculate the overall welfare effect) would sum over cross-price terms from the remaining twenty-four countries. The calculated standard errors of this sum tend to be very large – rendering virtually all the estimates of cross-price effects to be insignificantly different

implying that the proportional trade-creation impact of a PTA is assumed *identical* for all countries inside the bloc and, similarly, that the proportional impact of trade diversion is *identical* for all countries outside the bloc. In the context of the questions that this book is attempting to address, it should be readily evident that these assumptions would be far from innocuous. Finally, it cannot be rightly claimed that the gravity model can be used to estimate the impact of prospective trade blocs – in contrast to the methodology proposed herein that handles the estimation of potential preferential liberalization with equal ease. For criticisms of the gravity methodology on this point, see Hummels (1997) and Srinivasan (1997).

from zero. Because our final interest is in estimating, for each partner country, the value of the own-price and the cross-price effect (aggregated over the countries in the rest of the world in each case) we follow instead, the approach taken in some classic studies in international trade in estimating trade elasticities (e.g., Hickman and Lau [1973], Goldstein and Khan [1978], and Geraci and Prewo [1982]) of aggregating the rest of the world into a single unit. Thus, we estimate "triad" systems by splitting up the world into the home country, the partner country, and the rest of the world. Equation (13) then gives us a three-equation system to be estimated.[33,34]

In estimating the demand system, we have to consider the additional issues of simultaneity bias and measurement error in the righthand side variables – both of which could imply a correlation between the regressors and the error terms. Simultaneity bias may arise if the home country is not "small" in the trade theoretic sense, so that a change in

---

[33] As is the usual practice, to avoid the singularity that the adding-up constraint imposes, we drop one equation: here, the equation for the rest of the world.

[34] Thus, for each of the twenty-four partner countries considered in this analysis, we estimate a three-equation demand system with one equation representing the United States, one for that particular country, and one for the rest of the world.

its tariffs on imports would result in a change in the border prices of its imports. Measurement error may arise because the prices included on the righthand side are unit values rather than actual prices. This problem of the possible correlation between the regressors and the error terms is dealt with by using the method of instrumental variables. In particular, (13) is estimated jointly with four reduced-form "instrument equations" (one each for the endogenous variables on the righthand side of [13]): prices of the home country, the partner country, the rest of the world, and the real income term.[35] The endogenous variables are specified to be functions of exogenous variables in the system in the following traditional manner (e.g., see Bowden and Turkington [1984] and Newey [1986]):

$$x_j = \sum_k \beta_k X_k + \epsilon_j \qquad (17)$$

The lefthand side variables in (17) are the endogenous regressors in (13). On the righthand side are the exogenous variables: growth rates of home-country income and

---

[35] Note that we take the tariff levels themselves to be exogenously determined. Considering the endogeneity of tariffs themselves, as in the important paper of Trefler (1993), is outside the scope of this book.

*aggregate wage* rates in the partner country, in the four major trading partners other than the partner country and at home.[36]

Assuming that the errors of the spending equations (13) and the reduced-form (instrumenting) equations (17) have a joint normal distribution with zero mean and constant covariance matrix, we can estimate the demand system with the method of Maximum Likelihood (ML) – reliance on which allows the direct incorporation of the restrictions associated with consumer-demand theory. Likelihood ratio tests (discussed further in the next chapter) allow the testing of these restrictions and also the possible exogeneity of the righthand side variables in (13).

Using price and quantity information for each of these three groups, parameter estimates for the own- and cross-price effects can then be obtained. Plugging these into the righthand side of (10) gives an estimate of the overall welfare effect, which can then be compared with corresponding values for preferential tariff reduction with respect to other

---

[36] Because trade volumes of the partners with the home country relative to domestic GDP tend to be fairly small fractions, the exogeneity of the aggregate wage rate is not much of a concern. Statistical tests for the validity of the instruments used in the equations are discussed in Chapter 5.

countries. Comparing the welfare effect across countries, each at a different level of geographic proximity to the home country, allows us to test the natural trading partners theory.

## 4.3  Data and Estimation Results

### 4.3.1  Data

For this estimation, we need *bilateral* price and quantity information on imports from trading partners as well as wage rates in all of the partner countries. The present analysis employs U.S. imports data for the period 1965–1995 obtained from the U.N. Statistics Division in New York. This data set provides time-series information on import values measured in U.S. dollars, Cost, Insurance, and Freight (CIF), and separately on quantities of trade flows at the three-digit level. Information on bilateral tariff rates is also required; the *bilateral* customs collection rate was used here as the tariff measure. Data on customs collections for the period 1990–1995 were obtained directly from U.S. Customs. For the years 1964–1989, data were gathered from the U.S. Department of Commerce Publication FT 990. Wage data were obtained from International Labor Organization (ILO) and national accounts publications for the corresponding years.

Aggregate bilateral price indices were constructed[37] using the unit values that are implied by the U.N. data. For robustness, two aggregate price indices were used: the Fisher Ideal Index,[38] recommended by Fisher (1927), and the Laspeyeres Index. Aggregate quantity series were constructed by deflating aggregate trade flows with the corresponding price indices.[39] For consumption of domestically produced goods,

[37] If multilateral price indices were to be used instead, these could be directly obtained from the IMF's International Financial Statistics Handbooks. However, bilateral export price indices are a more accurate measure. Often, for single years, changes in bilateral prices are quite different in magnitude (and sometimes in sign) from changes in multilateral prices.

[38] As discussed in Fisher (1927), the Fisher Ideal Index, which is the geometric mean of the Laspeyeres and the Paasche indices, is "ideal" because it meets two tests for ideal indices set by Fisher: the time-reversal test and the factor-reversal test. Fisher showed that any index multiplied by its "time antithesis" would yield a new index that would meet the time-reversal test. Correspondingly, any index that was multiplied by its "factor antithesis" yielded a new index that met the factor antithesis test. Because Laspeyeres and Paasche are both time and factor antitheses of each other, multiplying them together yields an index – the Fisher Ideal Index – that meets both tests.

[39] In arriving at the results reported in this book, we constructed price indices using all available price data for any trade basket and then applied that price to the entire basket. The results are robust, however, to other methods of constructing price indices – such as those involving interpolation over missing values, the use of "chain indices" to take into account the changing composition of export baskets, and others.

the Consumer Price Index (CPI) was used as the price measure. U.S. purchases of domestically produced goods are measured as Gross National Product (GNP) minus exports.

## 4.3.2  Estimation Results

Tables 4.1 and 4.2 report the estimates of the own- and cross-price effects of U.S. preferential tariff reduction with respect to twenty-four different countries obtained by Full Information Maximum Likelihood (FIML) estimation of the demand system and using the Laspeyeres Index and the Fisher Ideal Index as the price indices, respectively. The corresponding elasticities, calculated using beginning of period budget shares, are also reported in Tables 4.1 and 4.2.

As shown in Tables 4.1 and 4.2, all estimates of the cross-price (trade diversion) effects are positive, indicating that the rest of the world's output and the partner country's output were substitutes and, therefore, that preferential tariff reductions would result in some trade diversion. The restriction that cross-price effects in the twenty-four cases were jointly zero was firmly rejected by the data,[40] suggesting

---

[40] The relevant likelihood test statistics were 83.12 and 77.66 for estimation with the Laspeyeres and Fisher Ideal Indices, respectively. The critical value at the 5 percent level for the $\chi^2$ with twenty-four degrees of freedom (the number of additional restrictions) is 36.42.

**Table 4.1.** *ML Estimates of Own- and Cross-Price Effects: Laspeyeres Index**

| Country | Cross-Price Effect: $(\pi_{ij}) \times 10^3$ | Cross-Price Elasticity: $(\frac{\pi_{ij}}{\omega_j})$ | Own-Price Effect: $(\pi_{ij}) \times 10^3$ | Own-Price Elasticity: $(\frac{\pi_{ij}}{\omega_j})$ | Welfare $\frac{HdW}{Y} \times 10^6$ | $R^2$ Partner |
|---|---|---|---|---|---|---|
| Argentina | 0.18 | 1.09 | −0.24 | −1.44 | 1.48 | 0.07 |
|  | (0.05) | (0.32) | (0.08) | (0.46) | (1.61) |  |
| Australia | 0.28 | 0.65 | −0.48 | −1.11 | 5.12 | 0.21 |
|  | (0.07) | (0.17) | (0.08) | (0.18) | (2.22) |  |
| Belgium | 1.11 | 1.61 | −1.45 | −2.11 | 8.73 | 0.52 |
|  | (0.23) | (0.33) | (0.16) | (0.23) | (4.37) |  |
| Brazil | 0.99 | 1.38 | −0.68 | −0.95 | −7.94 | 0.23 |
|  | (0.16) | (0.22) | (0.27) | (0.38) | (4.79) |  |
| Canada | 7.17 | 1.06 | −11.20 | −1.66 | 103.16 | 0.57 |
|  | (1.49) | (0.22) | (1.55) | (0.23) | (42.25) |  |
| Chile | 0.36 | 1.26 | −0.35 | −1.22 | −0.26 | 0.28 |
|  | (0.03) | (0.09) | (0.04) | (0.14) | (0.78) |  |
| France | 0.62 | 0.72 | −1.53 | −1.78 | 23.30 | 0.17 |
|  | (0.25) | (0.29) | (0.19) | (0.22) | (7.50) |  |
| Germany | 1.56 | 0.83 | −3.00 | −1.59 | 36.86 | 0.1 |
|  | (0.41) | (0.22) | (0.29) | (0.15) | (11.85) |  |
| Honduras | 0.00 | 0.00 | −0.09 | −0.88 | 2.17 | 0.14 |
|  | (0.03) | (0.31) | (0.04) | (0.43) | (0.87) |  |
| Hong Kong | 0.12 | 0.25 | −2.98 | −6.21 | 73.19 | 0.15 |
|  | (0.30) | (0.63) | (0.17) | (0.35) | (7.91) |  |
| Indonesia | 2.40 | 10.42 | −0.97 | −4.21 | −36.61 | 0.27 |
|  | (0.35) | (1.53) | (0.27) | (1.17) | (6.07) |  |
| Jamaica | 0.03 | 0.14 | −0.11 | −0.64 | 2.18 | 0.12 |
|  | (0.04) | (0.23) | (0.02) | (0.14) | (1.22) |  |
| Japan | 8.40 | 2.49 | −17.68 | −5.23 | 237.56 | 0.29 |
|  | (2.10) | (0.62) | (2.02) | (0.60) | (65.93) |  |
| Korea | 2.10 | 29.37 | −1.40 | −19.58 | −17.92 | 0.29 |
|  | (0.23) | (3.16) | (0.34) | (4.76) | (6.50) |  |
| Mexico | 3.13 | 3.51 | −4.11 | −4.61 | 25.09 | 0.03 |
|  | (0.50) | (0.56) | (0.79) | (0.89) | (12.38) |  |

**Table 4.1** *(Continued)*

| Country | Cross-Price Effect: $(\pi_{ij}) \times 10^3$ | Cross-Price Elasticity: $(\frac{\pi_{ij}}{\omega_j})$ | Own-Price Effect: $(\pi_{ij}) \times 10^3$ | Own-Price Elasticity: $(\frac{\pi_{ij}}{\omega_j})$ | Welfare $\frac{H dW}{Y} \times 10^6$ | $R^2$ Partner |
|---|---|---|---|---|---|---|
| New Zealand | 0.04 | 0.22 | −0.11 | −0.62 | 1.79 | 0.17 |
| | (0.02) | (0.11) | (0.03) | (0.17) | (0.97) | |
| Peru | 0.26 | 0.78 | −0.08 | −0.24 | −4.61 | 0.19 |
| | (0.06) | (0.17) | (0.03) | (0.09) | (1.48) | |
| Phillipines | 0.11 | 0.21 | −0.58 | −1.13 | 12.03 | 0.27 |
| | (0.08) | (0.17) | (0.06) | (0.11) | (2.36) | |
| South Africa | 0.40 | 1.30 | −0.50 | −1.62 | 2.56 | 0.33 |
| | (0.10) | (0.33) | (0.08) | (0.24) | (2.84) | |
| Switzerland | 0.16 | 0.38 | −0.50 | −1.17 | 8.70 | 0.11 |
| | (0.08) | (0.19) | (0.07) | (0.16) | (2.90) | |
| Taiwan | 1.39 | 11.05 | −6.20 | −49.28 | 123.13 | 0.49 |
| | (0.75) | (5.96) | (0.08) | (0.64) | (13.95) | |
| Thailand | 0.18 | 3.33 | −0.52 | −9.61 | 8.70 | 0.23 |
| | (0.10) | (1.85) | (0.06) | (1.11) | (1.11) | |
| Turkey | 0.03 | 0.23 | −0.10 | −0.88 | 1.89 | 0.24 |
| | (0.05) | (0.47) | (0.01) | (0.04) | (1.29) | |
| UK | 0.79 | 0.40 | −3.61 | −1.84 | 72.19 | 0.07 |
| | (0.46) | (0.23) | (0.61) | (0.31) | (18.81) | |

* Figures in parentheses are standard errors, "$i$" denotes partner country and "$j$" denotes the rest of the world. Elasticities were calculated using beginning of period budget shares of the relevant partner country in each case. Thus the elasticity corresponding to the cross price elasticity is the proportional change in imports from the partner country due a reduction in tariffs on the rest of the world.

that fears regarding the trade diversion with PTAs are not misplaced.

All of the estimates of the own-price (trade-creation) effects are negative, suggesting that these FTAs can be

**Table 4.2.** *ML Estimates of Own- and Cross-Price Effects: Fisher Ideal Index*[*]

| Country | Cross-Price Effect: $(\pi_{ij}) \times 10^3$ | Cross-Price Elasticity: $(\frac{\pi_{ij}}{\omega_j})$ | Own-Price Effect: $(\pi_{ii}) \times 10^3$ | Own-Price Elasticity: $(\frac{\pi_{ii}}{\omega_i})$ | Welfare $\frac{H\,dW}{Y} \times 10^6$ | $R^2$ Partner |
|---|---|---|---|---|---|---|
| Argentina | 0.21 | 1.27 | −0.43 | −2.59 | 5.63 | 0.04 |
|  | (0.06) | (0.37) | (0.11) | (0.66) | (1.72) |  |
| Australia | 0.20 | 0.46 | −0.41 | −0.95 | 5.38 | 0.07 |
|  | (0.07) | (0.17) | (0.08) | (0.18) | (2.18) |  |
| Belgium | 0.40 | 0.58 | −0.93 | −1.35 | 13.57 | 0.44 |
|  | (0.20) | (0.29) | (0.10) | (0.15) | (4.60) |  |
| Brazil | 0.56 | 0.78 | −0.39 | −0.55 | −4.35 | 0.02 |
|  | (0.10) | (0.15) | (0.19) | (0.27) | (2.93) |  |
| Canada | 6.31 | 0.93 | −15.03 | −2.22 | 223.22 | 0.46 |
|  | (2.14) | (0.32) | (3.00) | (0.44) | (48.84) |  |
| Chile | 0.38 | 1.32 | −0.35 | −1.22 | −0.77 | 0.57 |
|  | (0.03) | (0.11) | (0.01) | (0.03) | (0.80) |  |
| France | 0.97 | 1.12 | −1.73 | −2.01 | 19.58 | 0.39 |
|  | (0.25) | (0.29) | (0.21) | (0.24) | (7.47) |  |
| Germany | 1.39 | 0.74 | −2.59 | −1.37 | 30.72 | 0.88 |
|  | (0.39) | (0.21) | (0.23) | (0.12) | (18.34) |  |
| Honduras | 0.06 | 0.61 | −0.13 | −1.34 | 1.82 | 0.01 |
|  | (0.26) | (2.69) | (0.05) | (0.51) | (6.67) |  |
| Hong Kong | 0.00 | 0.01 | −2.47 | −5.15 | 63.11 | 0.47 |
|  | (0.28) | (0.58) | (0.17) | (0.35) | (7.91) |  |
| Indonesia | 1.20 | 5.21 | −1.00 | −4.34 | −5.12 | 0.07 |
|  | (0.34) | (1.47) | (0.25) | (1.09) | (5.68) |  |
| Jamaica | 0.02 | 0.14 | −0.11 | −0.64 | 2.20 | 0.08 |
|  | (0.04) | (0.24) | (0.02) | (0.14) | (1.24) |  |
| Japan | 5.85 | 1.73 | −18.63 | −5.52 | 327.16 | 0.43 |
|  | (2.00) | (0.59) | (2.10) | (0.62) | (68.83) |  |
| Korea | 1.88 | 26.29 | −1.24 | −17.34 | −16.38 | 0.06 |
|  | (0.22) | (3.04) | (0.35) | (4.90) | (6.49) |  |
| Mexico | 2.17 | 2.43 | −4.60 | −5.16 | 62.21 | 0.15 |
|  | (0.47) | (0.52) | (0.53) | (0.59) | (14.18) |  |

**Table 4.2 (Continued)**

| Country | Cross-Price Effect: $(\pi_{ij}) \times 10^3$ | Cross-Price Elasticity: $(\frac{\pi_{ij}}{\omega_j})$ | Own-Price Effect: $(\pi_{ii}) \times 10^3$ | Own-Price Elasticity: $(\frac{\pi_{ii}}{\omega_i})$ | Welfare $\frac{HdW}{Y} \times 10^6$ | $R^2$ Partner |
|---|---|---|---|---|---|---|
| New Zealand | 0.04 | 0.22 | −0.14 | −0.78 | 2.56 | 0.20 |
|  | (0.02) | (0.11) | (0.04) | (0.20) | (1.07) |  |
| Peru | 0.24 | 0.72 | −0.09 | −0.25 | −3.97 | 0.06 |
|  | (0.07) | (0.20) | (0.05) | (0.15) | (1.73) |  |
| Phillipines | 0.02 | 0.04 | −0.48 | −0.93 | 11.80 | 0.38 |
|  | (0.08) | (0.17) | (0.06) | (0.11) | (1.79) |  |
| South Africa | 0.21 | 0.68 | −0.33 | −1.07 | 3.07 | 0.23 |
|  | (0.06) | (0.20) | (0.08) | (0.25) | (1.22) |  |
| Switzerland | 0.15 | 0.35 | −0.33 | −0.77 | 4.61 | 0.68 |
|  | (0.09) | (0.21) | (0.03) | (0.07) | (2.50) |  |
| Taiwan | 1.06 | 8.43 | −5.81 | −46.18 | 121.60 | 0.07 |
|  | (0.76) | (6.04) | (0.53) | (4.21) | (19.90) |  |
| Thailand | 0.12 | 2.16 | −0.85 | −15.71 | 18.76 | 0.03 |
|  | (0.18) | (3.33) | (0.09) | (1.57) | (3.74) |  |
| Turkey | 0.03 | 0.25 | −0.15 | −1.29 | 3.05 | 0.23 |
|  | (0.04) | (0.35) | (0.02) | (0.15) | (1.04) |  |
| UK | 0.65 | 0.33 | −3.00 | −1.53 | 60.16 | 0.42 |
|  | (0.47) | (0.24) | (0.64) | (0.33) | (17.63) |  |

* Figures in parentheses are standard errors, "$i$" denotes partner country and "$j$" denotes the rest of the world. Elasticities were calculated using beginning of period budget shares of the relevant partner country in each case. Thus the elasticity corresponding to the cross price elasticity is the proportional change in imports from the partner country due a reduction in tariffs on the rest of the world.

expected to have positive trade-creating effects as well.[41] A simple comparison of the point estimates of the own- and

[41] The FIML estimation was carried out without the imposition of any sign restrictions, even on the own-price effects.

cross-price effects themselves indicates that, in most cases (although there are a few exceptions), own-price effects dominate cross-price effects in magnitude. Thus, roughly speaking, in these cases, if initial tariffs on the partner country and the rest of the world were equal, trade creation would outweigh trade diversion *around this initial equilibrium*. Finally, the implied elasticities reported in Tables 4.1 and 4.2 are broadly in line with elasticity estimates reported in the literature (e.g., see the Goldstein and Khan [1984] contribution to the Handbook of International Economics, Vol. II).

Next, using the estimates of the own- and cross-price effects reported in Tables 4.1 and 4.2 and using (10), we construct the overall welfare effect per unit of output $-\frac{H dW_j}{Y}$ and the associated standard errors. Because the ultimate goal is to correlate the estimates of welfare change with variables that we are interested in, we do not wish to let *actual* bilateral tariff levels affect the estimate of welfare change. Thus, we compute these welfare effects by substituting in (1) the average tariff levels imposed by the United States in 1994 (i.e., having obtained our estimates of own- and cross-price effects, themselves estimated under the assumption that they are invariant to income and prices, we imagine a world in which initial tariff levels are the same against all

countries and construct estimates of welfare change resulting from preferential tariff reduction against partner countries with a unit reduction in tariffs starting from this initial
situation). Given the relative precision of estimates of own-
and cross-price effects as reported in Tables 4.1 and 4.2,
the estimates of welfare change are also overwhelmingly
significant.

To examine correlations with distance, the following regression was then run:

$$-\frac{H\,dW_j}{Y} = \alpha + \beta_1 (distance)_j + +\epsilon_j \qquad (18)$$

where the distance measure used was the bilateral direct-
line distance (measured in thousands of miles) used by
Frankel, Stein, and Wei (1996).

To see how the welfare effect was correlated with distance
after conditioning for the income levels of the partner countries (as suggested by proponents of the gravity approach),
the following equation was estimated:

$$-\frac{H\,dW_j}{Y} = \alpha + \beta_1 (distance)_j + \beta_2 (Income)_j + \epsilon_j \qquad (19)$$

where income levels were simply GDP levels (measured in
billions of dollars) directly obtained from the International
Financial Statistics.

The dependent variable in each case was estimated and not observed. Furthermore, the estimated standard errors associated with each of these observations on the dependent variable were different, raising the issue of heteroscedasticity. To correct for this, the method of Weighted Least Squares (WLS) was used. WLS estimates obtained by using the (inverse of the) estimated errors as weights are presented in Table 4.3.

As these results indicate, the correlation between welfare change from preferential tariff reduction and distance is statistically insignificant. We cannot reject the null that distance does not matter. This can also been seen rather easily in Figures 4.1 and 4.2, which plot the welfare estimates against distance (both adjusted by the heteroscedasticity correction described previously). Clearly, no non-linear relationship between these variables is revealed in these plots either.

As shown in Table 4.3, the coefficient on distance remains insignificant even after conditioning on the partner's income level. Thus, these tests are unable to find any evidentiary support for the natural trading partners idea in U.S. data.

One issue arises due to the fact that the estimates of welfare changes are, strictly speaking, valid only for small changes around the initial equilibrium. To see why this is important, assume that we start with equal tariffs against

Table 4.3. *Testing the Natural Trade Partners Hypothesis*[†]

| Equation | Welfare Change vs | Laspeyeres Index WLS | Fisher Ideal Index WLS |
|---|---|---|---|
| | | Preferential Tariff Reduction | |
| 18 | Distance | −0.16 | −0.08 |
| | | (0.8) | (0.15) |
| 19 | Distance | −0.16 | −0.05 |
| | and | (0.8) | (0.15) |
| | Income | −1.80 | −8.00 |
| | | (13.00) | (9.90) |
| 20 | Import Volume | 0.50 | 0.37 |
| | | (0.65) | (0.59) |
| | | Preferential Tariff Reduction to Zero | |
| 18 | Distance | −0.05 | −0.08 |
| | | (0.13) | (0.11) |
| 19 | Distance | −0.05 | −0.06 |
| | and | (0.14) | (0.12) |
| | Income | 0.27 | −6.58 |
| | | (10.03) | (7.99) |
| 20 | Import Volume | −0.06 | −0.29 |
| | | (0.48) | (0.50) |

[†] Figures in parentheses are standard errors. Distance measured in thousands of miles, Income in trillions of US dollars and volume of trade in billions of dollars. The left hand side measuring welfare change in every case is $10^6$ times the real income change (due to a unit reduction in tariff) measured per unit U.S. income, i.e., $\frac{H dw}{Y} *$ $10^6$. Regressions were run using 1994 income and volume of trade data. For easy comparability, the second set of results, representing correlations with total preferential reduction in tariffs to zero, are per *unit* reduction in partner country tariffs.

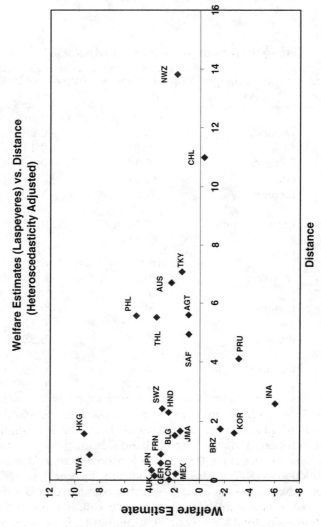

Figure 4.1 *Welfare Changes and Distance: Laspeyres Index*

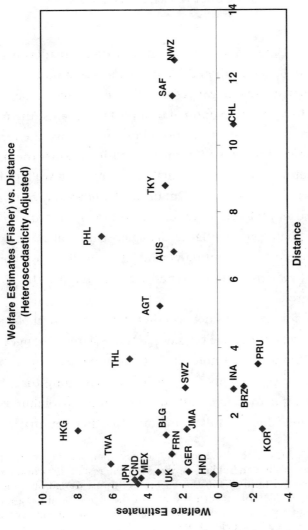

Figure 4.2 *Welfare Changes and Distance: Fisher Ideal Index*

B and C. Note from (10) that even if trade creation is estimated to be larger than trade diversion – assuming that $\pi_{ii}$ is estimated to be negative and $\pi_{ij}$ is estimated to be positive – there exists an optimal positive tariff against the partner country for any given (positive) tariff against the rest of the world. It follows that lowering tariffs against the partner country below this optimal tariff implies a welfare loss relative to this optimum.[42] In principle, however, countries engaged in preferential reduction in tariffs are required to reduce these preferential tariffs against the partner all the way to zero.[43] Computing welfare changes from total preferential tariff reduction (to zero) would require this to be considered.

Therefore, we consider whether the results would be significantly altered if we considered these "large" changes instead. It is useful to note, first, that the Slutsky own- and cross-price coefficients were estimated assuming that they are *invariant* to prices and income. Thus, to obtain welfare change due to a full reduction in partner-country tariffs

---

[42] Thus, Tables 4.1 and 4.2 roughly suggest that, starting from equal tariffs initially and holding tariff against the rest of the world fixed, the optimal tariff of the United States against Canada is roughly a third of its tariff against the rest of the world. Reducing tariffs against Canada below this level would then be welfare-decreasing.

[43] As stipulated in Article XXIV of the GATT.

to zero, we can integrate both sides of (10) over the relevant interval. The calculation is considerably simplified by assuming that the term "H" and income are constant over this interval.[44] Regression results for (18), (19), and (20) with this *total* welfare change on the lefthand side instead are presented in Table 4.3. The non-correlation with distance remains, again, even after controlling for income levels.[45]

---

[44] To see that this is not a bad approximation for the purposes at hand, note that "H" is closely related to the inverse of the marginal utility of income and measures the actual expenditure incurred, at world prices, for a unit increase in welfare. Imports overall are less than 10 percent of U.S. consumption. Of this, imports from any one country are less than about 20 percent (and only for the highest cases – Canada and Japan), implying that consumption of imports from any partner country are always less than about 2 percent of overall consumption. Thus, ignoring the impact of changes in tariffs on this good should not alter "H" by much. For the same reasons, as well as from the magnitudes of the estimates of the overall effect in Tables 4.1 and 4.2, it is easy to see that income changes themselves from preferential tariff reduction against any one partner country are not large relative to the base level of U.S. income.

[45] The non-correlation with distance persists even if (17), (18), and (19) are estimated separately by breaking the sample into two even periods and estimating separately for, say, developed country and developing country trade partners – thereby alleviating somewhat concerns that factors like biases in our price indices due to, say, underlying quality changes may be driving the results.

To summarize the results, then: First, we obtain significant estimates of trade creation and trade diversion associated with preferential tariff liberalization against various partner countries. Second, we find the correlation between the overall welfare effect and distance to be statistically insignificant and are, therefore, unable to reject the null that "distance does not matter" – with and without conditioning on income levels. Thus, this analysis of U.S. data does not find any evidentiary support for the natural trading partners idea.

— ✦ **CHAPTER FIVE** ✦ —

# Preferential Trading and Multilateralism

I n the recent revival of interest in PTAs, academic and policy discussions have been dominated by debates over the question of the impact of PTAs on the success of the multilateral process. Many have argued that multilateralism is too slow and inefficient a way of getting to the commonly held ideal of global free trade and that PTAs offer a quicker and surer way. In this context, interesting political-economy-theoretic questions relating to the interaction between bilateral agreements and multilateralism have been raised: Are there incentives for FTAs to keep expanding with more members so as to move toward multilateral free trade eventually, or will there be incentives instead to keep new members out?

To get to the question of the interaction between bilateral agreements and multilateralism with which this chapter is concerned, it is important to identify the factors that influence the determination of trade policy. Modeling the full range and relative magnitudes of these factors is a difficult task. It is, however, obvious that producers and producer interests play a strong role in determining trade-policy outcomes. Therefore, we start by describing a rather simple political economy framework in which the role of producers is decisive in determining the choice of reciprocal tariff-reducing arrangements. Trade policy is driven by the gains or losses of domestic firms under the different trade arrangements being considered. Alternate political economy frameworks are subsequently considered.

## 5.1 Endogenous PTAs and Multilateralism: A Lobbying Model

The formal model presented herein is a simple extension of the Brander-Krugman (1983) model. In Vinerian fashion and without loss of generality, the world is split into country $X$, country $Y$ (where $X$ and $Y$ are the potential partners in a bilateral arrangement), and the rest of the world, denoted by $Z$. There is a single good produced by firms from each country. The market structure is one of imperfect competition, with oligopolistic firms producing goods that are perfect substitutes for each other. The markets in the different countries are assumed to be segmented. The equilibrium concept is that of Cournot-Nash. We follow Dixit (1984) in assuming that firms do not incur any transportation costs in supplying the good abroad but that such costs are prohibitive for any third-party arbitrageurs. As in Brander and Krugman (1983), it is also assumed that a competitively produced numeraire good also exists and that it is freely traded. This numeraire good is transferred across countries to settle the balance of trade.

To facilitate the analysis, the notation is set up as follows: Let $i = X, Y, Z$ and $j = X, Y, Z$ be country indices. Then, let

$q_j^i$ = the quantity supplied by a single firm from country $i$ in country $j$'s markets

$P_j$ = the equilibrium price of the good in country $j$'s markets

$\pi_j^i$ = the profits made by any firm from country $i$ in country $j$'s markets

$t_j^i$ = the specific tariff imposed by country $j$ on imports from $i$

$n_i$ = number of firms in $i$

$n$ = $n_x + n_y + n_z$ is the total number of firms

It is assumed that there are no fixed costs of production and that marginal costs are constant at $c$ in terms of the numeraire good. Aggregate utility in country $j$ is assumed to take the form

$$U_j(K, Q_j) = K + \left(A_j Q_j - Q_j^2/2\right)$$

where $K$ denotes the consumption of the competitively produced numeraire good and where $Q_j = \Sigma_i n_i q_j^i$ denotes the total sales of the oligopolistically produced good in country $j$'s markets by firms from $X$, $Y$, and $Z$.

The price of this good in country $j$ is, therefore, a linear function of the total output

$$P_j = A_j - Q_j \tag{1}$$

Uniform non-discriminatory tariffs are initially assumed to be applied by all countries on imports from other countries. Therefore, to start with,

$$t_j^i = \begin{cases} t & \text{if } i \neq j \\ 0 & \text{if } i = j \end{cases}$$

In the usual manner, these tariffs simply add on to marginal costs of firms, whose effective marginal costs of exports then become $c + t$. Each firm regards each country as a separate market and, therefore, chooses its optimal quantity for each country separately. Under the Cournot assumption, firms are assumed to be maximizing profits taking other firms' outputs as given with all firms choosing their quantities simultaneously. Firms from country $i$, choosing the quantity to supply in country $j$, therefore solve the following problem:

$$\max_{q^i_j} \pi^i_j = q^i_j \left[ A_j - Q_j - (c + t^i_j) \right]$$

This yields

$$q^i_j = \left[ \Theta_j + \left( \frac{\Sigma_k n_k t^k_j}{n+1} \right) - t^i_j \right] \tag{2}$$

where $\Theta_j = (A_j - c)/(n+1)$ and $k = X, Y, Z$, as the Nash equilibrium output level.

From (2), we can derive the following comparative statics results that help establish the basic intuition of the model. First,

$$\frac{dq^y_x}{dt^y_x} = \left( \frac{n_y}{n+1} \right) - 1 < 0 \tag{3}$$

This implies that as tariffs are reduced by $X$ on the partner country $Y$, the quantity supplied by the firms from $Y$ in $X$'s markets increases Second, we have

$$\frac{dq^z_x}{dt^y_x} = \left( \frac{n_y}{n+1} \right) > 0 \tag{4}$$

That is, the opposite is true for $Z$'s firms: As tariffs are re-duced by $X$ on imports from $Y$, the quantity supplied by firms from $Z$ in $X$'s market decreases. Finally,

$$\frac{dq_x^x}{dt_x^y} = \left(\frac{n_y}{n+1}\right) > 0 \qquad (5)$$

Thus, just as for $Z$'s firms, a reduction in tariffs by $X$ against $Y$ will decrease the quantity supplied by $X$'s firms in their own domestic markets.

From (1) and (2), it can also easily be seen that

$$\pi_j^i = \left[q_j^i\right]^2 \qquad (6)$$

It follows that with a change in tariffs, firm profits would change in the same direction as changes in equilibrium quantities sold by them, as given by equations (3), (4), and (5).

The political economy framework is one where produc-ers play a decisive role in shaping trade policy.[46] We have

---

[46] This may easily be understood to result from the public-good nature of political activity that is more easily provided by a concentrated group of producers rather than by large diffuse groups of consumers. The theoretical and empirical literature on the effectiveness of such interest groups in bending policy in a direction that is to their benefit is, of course, quite well developed by now. For the classic theoret-ical arguments, see Olson (1965), Stigler (1971), Peltzman (1976), and Becker (1983). O'Halloran (1994) provides a comprehensive survey.

in mind an agenda-setting government that considers both bilateral and multilateral reciprocal tariff reductions. Firms lobby[47] either for or against these proposed trade-regime changes depending on whether they would see an increase in their profits following a given change in regime. For instance, a proposed bilateral arrangement between countries $X$ and $Y$ will be supported by firms from $X$ if they see a *net* increase in their profits following this bilateral arrangement. With a reciprocal reduction in tariffs, firms from either country would see a reduction in profits in their home market and an increase in profits made abroad (from [3] and [5]). In our segmented markets and constant-costs framework, firm profits in any single market are independent of profits in other markets, and we can separately compute the losses in the import-competing side and the gains on the exporting side. Overall, because in this framework the same firms constitute both the exporting sector and the import-competing

[47] Similar to the well-known Findlay and Wellisz (1982) model of trade-policy determination, the actual lobbying process is not explicitly modeled here and is left as somewhat of a black box. See also Grossman and Helpman (1994) whose theory of endogenous protection formally describes the interaction between firms and organized lobbies and, further, Mitra (1999) who derives endogenously the structure of organized lobbies. For a survey discussion of the empirical validity of such interest-group theories of trade policy determination, see Gawande and Krishna (2003).

sector, firms from each country would either all gain or all lose following any trade-policy change. If the gains are greater than the losses, it is assumed that the proposed trade-policy change is implemented. Alternately, if exporting firms and import-competing firms were to be modeled separately, this assumption regarding the determination of trade policy would be equivalent to assuming that the winners would be willing to lobby the government to the full extent of their expected gains, whereas the losers would be willing to lobby the government to the full extent of their losses. Thus, if the winners gain more than the losers lose, the proposed change will be implemented.

This analysis of the conditions under which the three countries would reduce tariffs against each other (preferentially or otherwise) is, therefore, carried out by looking exclusively at the impact of various trade arrangements on relevant producer profits.[48]

The remainder of this analysis is structured as follows: We first examine the conditions under which a bilateral

[48] While this assumption has the benefit of yielding tractable closed-form solutions, the results presented here can be generated under more general specifications of the political economy process *inter alia*. In Appendix 5.6 we present a numerical example in which consumer interests play a role in the political process as well and in which the initial tariffs are endogenously determined.

arrangement will be entered into by $X$ and $Y$. We then examine the impact on the incentives for multilateral liberalization vis-à-vis the rest of the world, $Z$, by comparing the incentives for such a liberalization both before and after the bilateral arrangement is in place.

## 5.1.1 Bilateral Tariff Reductions

Article XXIV of the GATT Articles of Agreement permits CUs and FTAs. However, these preferential arrangements are sanctioned only as long as "duties and other regulations of commerce" on "substantially all trade" are eliminated. Here, the GATT rules are interpreted as requiring that goods be freely traded between the parties to the agreement. Accordingly, a bilateral arrangement between $X$ and $Y$ implies that $t_y^x$ and $t_x^y$ have to be set equal to zero.

Let $_Bq_j^i$ denote the equilibrium quantities that would be sold once the bilateral arrangement is in place and let $_B\pi_j^i$ denote the corresponding profits.

Because producer profits are decisive, for a bilateral arrangement to be supported in country $X$ and country $Y$, we need,

$$\Sigma_j\left(_B\pi_j^x\right) > \Sigma_j\pi_j^x \quad \text{and} \quad \Sigma_j\left(_B\pi_j^y\right) > \Sigma_j\pi_j^y$$

that is, we need

$$\Sigma_j\left(_Bq_j^x\right)^2 > \Sigma_j\left(q_j^x\right)^2 \quad \text{and} \quad \Sigma_j\left(_Bq_j^y\right)^2 > \Sigma_j\left(q_j^y\right)^2 \quad (7)$$

Simplifying these expressions gives us Proposition 1.

**Proposition 1.** A bilateral arrangement will only be supported by $X$ and $Y$ if

$$\left[q_x^x + _Bq_x^x\right]n_y < \left[q_y^x + _Bq_y^x\right](1 + n_z + n_y) \quad (8)$$

and

$$\left[q_y^y + _Bq_y^y\right]n_x < \left[q_x^y + _Bq_x^y\right](1 + n_z + n_x) \quad (9)$$

These conditions can be derived directly using (2), (7), and our assumptions regarding the symmetry of initial tariffs (see Appendix 5.2). They can be interpreted, roughly, as requiring the sales in the partner country to be sufficiently large relative to home-country sales for the agreement to be supported by the home country. The intuition here is clear: With a bilateral arrangement, better access is gained to the partner's market; the larger the partners market, the greater the gains. What is lost, however, is market share in your own market. The gains have to be greater than the losses for the arrangement to be supported. This gives us conditions that require the size of the partner's market to be sufficiently large relative to the size of the domestic market for the arrangement to be supported.

Condition (8) has to hold for $X$ to support the arrangement. In addition to the terms denoting the sales in $Y$'s market, the term $(1 + n_z + n_y)$ enters on the righthand side of this condition and the term $n_y$ enters on the lefthand side of this equation, which can be interpreted as follows. The gains in $Y$'s market come from two sources:

(1) The reduction in the tariffs imposed by $Y$ against $X$, which reduces their effective marginal costs in $Y$ from $c + t$ to $c$. This is the direct effect. This accounts for the "1" in the $1 + n_y + n_z$ term.

(2) The reduction in marginal costs of $X$'s firms relative to firms from $Y$ and $Z$ shifts the equilibrium quantities in $X$'s favor. Firms from $X$ gain a competitive advantage over the $n_y$ firms from $Y$ and the $n_z$ firms from $Z$. This is the strategic effect. This accounts for the $n_y + n_z$ in the $1 + n_y + n_z$ term. The larger the number of firms $(n_y + n_z)$ over which firms from $X$ gain a strategic advantage, the greater the strategic effect.

In their own domestic market, there is no direct effect on $X$'s firms because their effective marginal costs remain the same. There is a strategic loss relative to firms from $Y$

(whose marginal costs in $X$ similarly fall from $c + t$ to $c$), which accounts for the $n_y$ term on the lefthand side of the equation. Condition (9), which may be interpreted, *mutatis mutandis*, in exactly the same manner as (8), needs to hold for $Y$ to support the bilateral arrangement.

One question that naturally arises is whether conditions (8) and (9) could hold simultaneously. In other words, could $X$'s market be sufficiently large relative to $Y$ and could $Y$'s market be sufficiently large relative to $X$'s market at the same time? To answer this question, we first specify (8) and (9) in terms of the primitives: the parameters of the demand and cost functions. Using (2), these conditions can be rewritten as

$$\alpha_x < \frac{1}{2n_y}\alpha_y(2 + 2n_y + 2n_z) - 2tn_yn_z + t(n_z)^2$$
$$- t(n_y)^2 - t(1 + n_y)^2 \tag{10}$$

and

$$\alpha_y < \frac{1}{2n_x}\alpha_x(2 + 2n_x + 2n_z) - 2tn_xn_z + t(n_z)^2$$
$$- t(n_x)^2 - t(1 + n_x)^2 \tag{11}$$

where $\alpha_j = A_j - c$.[49] Equations (10) and (11) give us our second proposition.

**Proposition 2.** If conditions (10) and (11) are both satisfied by $(\alpha_x, \alpha_y, \alpha_z, n_x, n_y, n_z)$, they are necessarily satisfied by $(\alpha_x, \alpha_y, \alpha_z, n_x, n_y, n'_z) \; \forall \; n'_z > n_z$.

This is easily verified by examining the righthand side of conditions (10) and (11). Note that from (2), with initial trade being non-zero,

$$\alpha_x - tn_x = (n+1)q_x^y + t > 0$$

and

$$\alpha_y - tn_y = (n+1)q_y^x + t > 0$$

implying that the righthand sides of conditions (10) and (11) are increasing in $n_z$. With a larger number of firms from $Z$, both conditions are more likely to hold. The intuition for this result is as follows: With larger $n_z$, the number of firms over which firms from $X$ (in $Y$) and from $Y$ (in $X$) gain a

[49] It can easily be verified that equations (10) and (11) hold together for a wide range of parameter values (a numerical example is presented in Appendix 5.3).

strategic advantage is larger. The strategic effect (causing a larger diversion of sales away from the rest of the world's firms to partner-country firms) is, therefore, larger for both firms from $X$ selling in $Y$ and for firms from $Y$ selling in $X$.[50] This gives us a strong result: The larger the trade diversion[51] that would result from the preferential arrangement, the more likely it is that the arrangement will be supported by the partner countries.[52]

To better interpret conditions (8) and (9), it is useful to think of the case with $n_z = 0$. In this case, we (trivially) have no trade diversion. In $X$, firms from $Y$ take away market share only from the domestic firms. Similarly in $Y$, $X$'s firms take away market share only from $Y$'s firms. There is increased competition in both markets, implying that the strategic effect on net is negative in the absence of trade diversion. However, due to the direct effect (reduction in

---

[50] The signs of the direct and strategic effects discussed herein can be shown to hold for more general demand functions than the linear form considered. See Dixit (1986) for a discussion.

[51] That a larger number of firms in $Z$ translates into greater volume of trade diversion is shown in Appendix 5.5.

[52] Independent (and contemporaneous) work by Grossman and Helpman (1995) arrives at a conclusion that is similar in spirit: A preferential arrangement would be politically viable if it resulted in "enhanced protection" for partner-country firms.

effective marginal costs), it may still be possible for $X$ and $Y$ to both gain with the bilateral arrangement. To the extent that direct effects are large enough, they dominate the losses due to increased competition, and (10) and (11) are both satisfied. On the other hand, if strategic losses on net dominate the direct effects, firms from both countries see reduced profits and the bilateral arrangement is not established.

From this discussion, and comparing the lefthand and righthand sides of (8) and (9) when $n_z = 0$, it would also appear that, absent any trade diversion gains for partner-country firms, it would be the case that countries of roughly the same size would enter into bilateral arrangements. However, as discussed previously, to the extent that direct effects (gains) are dominated by strategic losses, (8) and (9) may, of course, not be satisfied even if the two countries are completely symmetrical. Most important – and this serves to highlight the role of trade diversion in this model – the diversion of trade away from the rest of the world relaxes both these conditions (as illustrated in Figure 5.1), thus permitting higher profits for firms from both countries even with asymmetry in partner-country sizes and the number of firms.

Figure 5.1 illustrates this point. XX represents (10) and YY represents (11) for any given number of firms from $Z$,

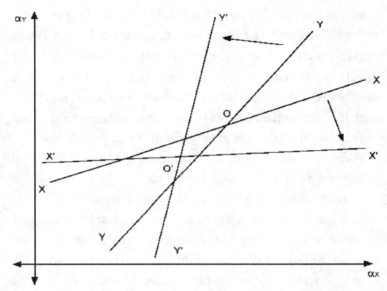

**Figure 5.1** *Trade Diversion and Preferential Liberalization*

$n_z$. X′X′ and Y′Y′ are the loci if the number of firms from $Z$ is $n'_z > n_z$. With $n_z$ firms, the bilateral arrangement will be supported by $X$ at all points above XX. The arrangement will be supported by $Y$ at all points below YY. The shaded area XOY is where both countries would support the bilateral arrangement. With $n'_z$ firms, X′O′Y′ is the area within which both $X$ and $Y$ would support the bilateral arrangement. Note that XOY is contained entirely within X′O′Y′. It can be easily verified that the loci shift in the manner indicated in Figure 5.1. The proof is in Appendix 5.4.

The welfare effects of the bilateral arrangement can be analyzed using the standard surplus measures. From Appendix 5.1, we know that overall world welfare increases. Importantly, however, due to trade diversion, welfare unambiguously decreases in the rest of the world (i.e., consumer surplus and tariff revenues stay the same while producer profits decrease – from [4] and [6]). Thus, the partner countries gain in sum. Producer profits increase (by [7]) and consumer surplus increases as well (because a larger quantity is sold in each market with any tariff reductions; see Appendix 5.1) for both partner countries. However, tariff revenues fall (because tariffs on imports from the partner reduce to zero and imports from the rest of the world are reduced). Because the partner countries gain in sum, in the symmetric case, clearly, producer and consumer gains dominate these tariff revenue losses. With some asymmetry, however, tariff revenue losses may outweigh consumer and producer gains for one of the partner countries whose welfare will consequently fall.[53]

[53] This result that politically supported, trade-diverting PTAs may result in welfare improvement for member countries, in contrast to the popular intuition regarding trade-diverting PTAs being

## 5.1.2 Multilateral Tariff Liberalization

Assuming that (10) and (11) are satisfied, and that a bilateral arrangement is in place between $X$ and $Y$, we now examine the incentives that $X$ and $Y$ face for multilateral tariff liberalization vis-à-vis $Z$. As stated herein, by multilateral liberalization, we mean an elimination of tariffs by all countries on imports from other countries. Prior to the bilateral arrangement, this implies an equal reduction in tariffs by $X$,

> welfare-decreasing, is similar though not entirely identical, of course, to the perfectly competitive cases as analyzed by Lipsey (1957, 1960), Bhagwati (1971), and Michaely (1976). These authors variously showed, in elaboration and partial contradiction of the classic analysis by Viner (1950, that the Vinerian intuition regarding trade diversion being welfare-decreasing resulted from the exclusion as in Viner's original analysis) of producer and consumer gains from the calculus. Thus, they showed that more general analysis of PTAs that permitted producer and consumer gains could easily result in welfare improvement even with trade diversion, just as in the present analysis. Additionally, in an important contribution that is closer in its workings to the present analysis due to its consideration of PTAS that involve *reciprocal* tariff reductions (in contrast to the analysis of Viner and most subsequent researchers who analyzed PTAs with *unilateral* preferential reductions instead), Wonnacott and Wonnacott (1981) have argued that, with reciprocity, the scope for terms of trade losses itself is reduced and we have an even greater possibility of welfare improvement even when the PTA is trade-diverting. The possibility of welfare reduction, particularly when countries are asymmetric remains, again, just as in the present analysis.

$Y$, and $Z$. After the bilateral arrangement between $X$ and $Y$, multilateral liberalization implies that $X$ and $Y$ eliminate their tariffs against a reciprocating $Z$ and that the tariffs imposed by $X$ on imports from $Y$ and vice versa continue to be zero.

Let

$$\Pi_x = \Sigma_j \pi_j^x$$

$$_B\Pi_x = \Sigma_j \left(_B\pi_j^x\right)$$

and

$$_M\Pi_x = \Sigma_j \left(_M\pi_j^x\right)$$

denote the total profits of a firm from $X$ prior to the bilateral arrangement, after the bilateral arrangement, and after total multilateral liberalization, respectively.

As a simplification, assume that the partner countries are identical – that is, that $A_x = A_y$ and $n_x = n_y$. This allows us to examine the effects of the bilateral arrangement on any one partner country (instead of having to carry out the analysis for both partner countries separately). Without any further loss of generality, we now only look at these effects on firms from $X$.

Consider first the increase in profits with multilateral liberalization before the bilateral arrangement:

$$_M\Pi_x - \Pi_x = \left(_M\pi_x^x - \pi_x^x\right) + \left(_M\pi_y^x - \pi_y^x\right)$$
$$+ \left(_M\pi_z^x - \pi_z^x\right) \qquad (12)$$

where

$$\left(_M\pi_x^x - \pi_x^x\right) = \text{gain in the domestic market} < 0$$
$$\left(_M\pi_y^x - \pi_y^x\right) = \text{gain in } Y\text{'s market} > 0$$

and

$$\left(_M\pi_z^x - \pi_z^x\right) = \text{gain in } Z\text{'s market} > 0$$

Next, consider the increase in profits with multilateral liberalization after a bilateral arrangement is in place between $X$ and $Y$:

$$_M\Pi_x - {_B}\Pi_x = \left(_M\pi_x^x - {_B}\pi_x^x\right) + \left(_M\pi_y^x - {_B}\pi_y^x\right)$$
$$+ \left(_M\pi_z^x - {_B}\pi_z^x\right) \qquad (13)$$

where

$$\left(_M\pi_x^x - {_B}\pi_x^x\right) = \text{gain in the domestic market} < 0$$
$$\left(_M\pi_y^x - {_B}\pi_y^x\right) = \text{gain in Y's market} < 0$$

and

$$\left(_M\pi_z^x - {_B}\pi_z^x\right) = \text{gain in } Z\text{'s market} > 0$$

We are finally interested in comparing $(_M\Pi_x - \Pi x)$ with $(_M\Pi_x - _B\Pi_x)$. Clearly, the change in profits in $Z$ (the third term in [12] and [13]) is the same, before and after the bilateral arrangement. The second term, the change in profits in $Y$, is positive in (12) and negative in (13). The first term is negative in both cases, but it is less negative in (13), due to the fact that with the bilateral arrangement, some market share is already lost by $X$'s firms to $Y$'s firms and with the multilateral reduction in tariffs, $X$'s firms have less to lose in their own domestic markets than they would have with direct multilateral liberalization. It may, therefore, appear that the sign of the difference between the righthand sides of (12) and (13) may have to be determined parametrically, depending on the relative magnitude of these two opposing factors. However, introducing (7) into (12) and (13) immediately resolves this and allows us to state that "politically supported" preferential arrangements necessarily reduce domestic incentives to seek multilateral tariff liberalization – that is $(_M\Pi_x - \Pi_x) - (_M\Pi_x - _B\Pi_x)$ is always $> 0$. This can be seen by noting, first, that

$$(_M\Pi_x - \Pi_x) - (_M\Pi_x - _B\Pi_x) = -(\Pi_x - _B\Pi_x)$$

and second, that from (7), for the bilateral arrangement to

be supported in the first place,

$$_B\Pi_x > \Pi_x$$

which readily gives us

$$(_M\Pi_x - \Pi_x) - (_M\Pi_x - _B\Pi_x) > 0$$

The point here is simply that the fact that the bilateral arrangement was supported by $X$ and $Y$ in the first place gives us information about the impact of the bilateral arrangement on multilateral liberalization incentives and helps us determine unambiguously that preferential arrangements reduce the incentives for multilateral liberalization.

Although it is now clear that these incentives will be reduced, we need to ask if these incentives would ever be reversed; that is, could multilateral liberalization that was initially feasible be rendered infeasible by the bilateral arrangement? This consideration gives us Proposition 3.

**Proposition 3.** Politically supported bilateral arrangements could critically reduce internal incentives for multilateral liberalization. That is, multilateral liberalization that was otherwise feasible could lose support due to a bilateral arrangement. This is more likely the larger the trade diversion associated with the bilateral arrangement.

For this, we need to see if the following conditions could hold together:

$$_M\Pi_x - \Pi_x > 0 \quad \text{and} \quad _M\Pi_x - {_B}\Pi_x < 0 \qquad (14)$$

With substantial algebraic manipulation, (14) can be rewritten as

$$h(n_z) < \alpha_z < g(n_z),$$

where

$$h(n_z) = \left(\frac{t}{2(1+n_z)}\right)\left[(n_y + n_z)^2 + (1 + n_y)^2\right.$$
$$\left. + (1 + n_z)^2\right] + \frac{\alpha_x(n_z - 1)}{(1 + n_z)}$$

and

$$g(n_z) = \left(\frac{t}{2(1+n_z)}\right)\left[2(n_z)^2 + (1 + n_z)^2\right] + \frac{2\alpha_x n_z}{(1 + n_z)}$$

as the condition under which the bilateral arrangement can render infeasible multilateral liberalization.

It is easily verified that

$$h(n_z) < g(n_z) \qquad (15)$$

and that

$$\frac{d(g(n_z) - h(n_z))}{dn_z} > 0 \qquad (16)$$

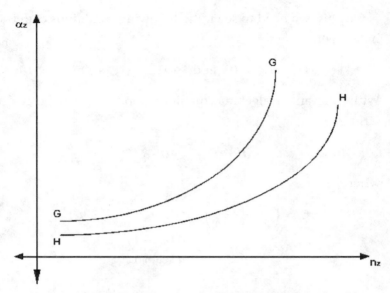

**Figure 5.2 *PTAs and Incentives for Multilateral Liberalization***

If $\alpha_z$ lies between $h(n_z)$ and $g(n_z)$, the bilateral arrangement would impede multilateral liberalization.[54]

Figure 5.2 illustrates this point by appropriately partitioning the $(\alpha_z, n_z)$ space. HH is the locus of points that

---

[54] Although the focus of this book is on internal incentives for multilateral liberalization, it could be that a bilateral arrangement between $X$ and $Y$ makes an initially uninterested $Z$ seek multilateral trade liberalization if the bilateral arrangement diverts a large amount of trade away from it; that is, if $\Pi_z >_M \Pi_z >_B \Pi_z$.

satisfy $h(n_z) = \alpha_z$ and GG is the locus of points that satisfy $g(n_z) = \alpha_z$. HH and GG, therefore, correspond to points at which multilateral liberalization is just feasible, initially and after the bilateral arrangement is in place, respectively. Initially, multilateral liberalization is feasible above HH and infeasible below. After the bilateral arrangement is in place, multilateral liberalization is feasible above GG and infeasible below. Therefore, between GG and HH, the bilateral arrangement would render infeasible multilateral liberalization. The intuition is as follows: For a given value of $n_z$, a larger $\alpha_z$ (a direct measure of the size of $Z$'s market) implies larger gains for both $X$ and $Y$ following a reciprocal reduction in tariffs against $Z$. After the bilateral arrangement is in place, for multilateral liberalization to be feasible, an even larger $\alpha_z$ is required. With multilateral liberalization, $Z$'s firms gain equal access to the markets in $X$ and $Y$. This eliminates the gains that $X$ and $Y$ had enjoyed due to the preferential access to each other's markets. A larger $\alpha_z$ is, therefore, required to offset this. This is why the GG locus is above the HH locus. Note also that with larger $n_z$, there is a wider range of values of $\alpha_z$ for which the bilateral arrangement would render multilateral liberalization infeasible. This follows directly from the fact that with larger $n_z$, the bilateral arrangement results in larger trade diversion gains for $X$ and $Y$

(Proposition 2), which would now be eliminated requiring even higher values of $\alpha_z$ for multilateral liberalization to still be supported by $X$ and $Y$. Therefore, the larger the trade diversion resulting from the PTA, the more likely it is that multilateral liberalization loses support.[55]

To summarize, our analysis of PTAs reaches two conclusions: (1) PTAs that divert trade away from the rest of the world are more likely to be supported politically; and (2) that such PTAs will reduce the incentives for multilateral liberalization. It is also shown that in some cases, this reduction in incentives could be critical: Multilateral liberalization that is initially feasible could be rendered infeasible by PTAs.

## 5.2  Endogenous PTAs and Multilateralism: A Median Voter Model

An elegant and alternate analysis of endogenous PTA formation in which the political economy process is assumed to be that of direct democracy (with voters voting over trade

---

[55] It is easy to show that if we started with four countries, $X$, Y, $R$, and $Z$, and considered bilateral arrangements in sequence (between $X$ and $Y$ first and then between $X$ and $Y$ and $R$), the GG curve would be pushed even higher following the second bilateral arrangement, resulting in a larger range of values of $\alpha_z$ and $n_z$ for which total multilateral liberalization would become infeasible.

policy) was provided by Levy (1997). Interestingly, while in this framework the motivations for countries to enter into PTAs are quite different from those discussed for the previous framework, Levy reaches similar conclusions about the interaction between bilateral agreements and multilateralism. Bilateral agreements may impede multilateral progress – that is, otherwise feasible multilateral agreements can be rendered infeasible by bilateral agreements.

The details of Levy's model are as follows. Consider a world in which there are three countries – A, B, and C – where A and B are potential partners in a PTA. Two types of goods are assumed to be produced in each of these countries: (1) a homogeneous good produced using capital and labor under constant returns to scale; and (2) a differentiated good of which many different varieties are produced, also using capital and labor, but under increasing returns to scale (with the market for this product characterized by monopolistic competition). Ownership of the factors of production is assumed to be uneven across individuals (i.e., all agents supply the same unit quantity of labor but differ in the amount of capital they own). The homogeneous good and the differentiated good are assumed to be produced using different factor intensities. Trade liberalization in this framework has two types of effects on an individual in the liberalizing economy. First, a move from autarky to trade increases the number of varieties that all individuals in the economy can consume. Second, as in the standard Heckscher–Ohlin model, trade involves changes in relative rewards to factors that would bring gains to or hurt an individual depending on the extent of that individual's relative ownership of those factors. The political process, as has already been mentioned, is one of direct democracy. Given the assumptions of the model, Levy shows that the voter with the median capital/labor ratio will be of primary importance because that voter will always be in the majority on any vote.

Now, consider first the economy of home country A under autarky. It is easy see that a median voter's utility in this country can be represented by the inverted U-shaped plot of utility level versus the economy's capital/labor endowment as shown in Figure 5.3. Here, the median voter's capital/labor (ownership) ratio is given by the point $k_m = K_m/L_m$. If the economy overall had the same capital/labor ratio as this median voter, the level of utility derived by the median voter is given by the point $U_m^{min}$. On the other hand, if the capital/labor ratio of the economy were, say, $k^A$, the agent would have a level of utility

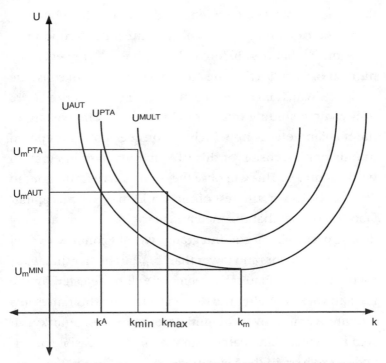

**Figure 5.3** *Median Voter Choices: PTA vs. Multilateral Free Trade*

$U_m^{AUT}$, which is higher than $U_m^{MIN}$ because this agent is now effectively able to trade with the rest of the country and benefit from this. Consider that A enters into a FTA with B, which is assumed for the purposes of the argument to have the same identical endowments and production technology as A. The capital/labor ratio of this integrated economy is the same as that of A before – that is, it is $k^A$. However, the number of varieties that the median voter in A can consume is higher, which increases his or her utility (with the entire utility curve shifting out from $U$ to $U^{PTA}$). The welfare of the median voter is now higher. Consider now a proposed multilateral extension of this PTA that involves integration with country C. This will raise the utility curve farther out to $U^{MULT}$. However, the rest of the world may have a capital/labor ratio such that the median voter's utility may actually drop. Specifically, if the integrated world economy overall has a capital/labor ratio lower than $k_{min}$ but higher than $k_{max}$, then such a multilateral agreement will be rejected by the median voter in A after the PTA, even though this represents an improvement over the initial situation (i.e., autarky). It is in this sense that bilateralism may impede feasible multilateral progress in the Levy model.[56]

---

[56] A similar finding is reached by McLaren (2002) who develops a theory of "insidious" regionalism. Here, private parties in member countries make investment decisions that make bloc member countries more specialized toward one another but make bloc and

## 5.2.1  Domino Effects

In reaching the conclusion that multilateral progress may be impeded by bilateral agreements, the two theoretical frameworks (Krishna [1998] and Levy [1997]) both consider incentives for member countries to expand PTAs. Baldwin (1995), on the other hand, examines incentives for non-members to want to enter into expanding PTAs. He argues that the incentives for non-members to join an existing FTA increase as the number of member countries in the agreement rise. The argument is a straightforward one. Imagine that non-members need to balance out the economic benefits of entry into the PTA (i.e., the benefit of gaining the preferential access) with other costs of entry (e.g., political costs). Consider now an initial equilibrium in which the non-member country is indifferent between joining and not joining. Other non-members with higher political costs may, on balance, have even less incentive to join the PTA. An exogenous shock that improves the level of integration of the PTA or the size of the PTA will now tip the balance for the marginal non-member in favor of joining. This, in turn, leads

non-bloc countries mutually less specialized, thus diminishing the ex-post demand for multilateral free trade.

to greater incentives for the remaining non-members – thus, the domino effect.[57]

The question of the interaction between multilateralism and preferential trade is a difficult one. Some of the research papers discussed suggest that PTAs may be an impediment to multilateral liberalization, others suggest otherwise.[58] This makes it difficult to reach robust policy conclusions with great certitude. The rapid proliferation of complex and over-lapping PTAs and the distortions that they bring to the trading system have led many economists to reassert strongly their faith in the multilateral process, for it is clear that elimination of multilateral barriers eliminates all incentives for preferential trading as well.

[57] Andriamananjara (2002) models jointly the incentives for members to expand existing FTAs and for non-members to join them, finding that the PTA will expand initially but will stop short of reaching global free trade. A similar finding is reached by Bond and Syropoulos (1996) in a somewhat different modeling framework.

[58] Indeed, other analysts arrive at even more ambivalent conclusions on this interaction. Thus, using the framework of self-enforcing trade agreements, Bagwell and Staiger (1997) investigate how multilateral behavior is impacted during the phase-in period for tariff reduction with PTAs and argue that the behavior of multilateral tariffs is both non-monotonic and dependent on whether the concerned PTA is an FTA or a CU. Further, Freund (2000), using a similar framework, finds that the incentives to form PTAs may well depend on the level of multilateral tariffs themselves. See Bohara, Gawande, and Sanguinetti (2004) and Limao (2004) for related empirical analyses.

# Appendices

## Chapter 2

### 2.1 GATT: Article XXIV and Understanding on the Interpretation of Article XXIV of the General Agreement on Tariffs and Trade 1994

GATT: Article XXIV

*Territorial Application – Frontier Traffic – Customs Unions and Free-Trade Areas*

1. The provisions of this Agreement shall apply to the metropolitan customs territories of the contracting parties and to any other customs territories in respect of which this Agreement has been accepted under Article XXVI or is being applied under Article XXXIII or pursuant to the Protocol of Provisional Application. Each

such customs territory shall, exclusively for the purposes of the territorial application of this Agreement, be treated as though it were a contracting party; *provided* that the provisions of this paragraph shall not be construed to create any rights or obligations as between two or more customs territories in respect of which this Agreement has been accepted under Article XXVI or is being applied under Article XXXIII or pursuant to the Protocol of Provisional Application by a single contracting party.

2. For the purposes of this Agreement, a customs territory shall be understood to mean any territory with respect to which separate tariffs or other regulations of commerce are maintained for a substantial part of the trade of such territory with other territories.

3. The provisions of this Agreement shall not be construed to prevent:

    (*a*) Advantages accorded by any contracting party to adjacent countries in order to facilitate frontier traffic;

    (*b*) Advantages accorded to the trade with the Free Territory of Trieste by countries contiguous to that territory, provided that such advantages are not in conflict with the Treaties of Peace arising out of the Second World War.

4. The contracting parties recognize the desirability of increasing freedom of trade by the development, through voluntary agreements, of closer integration between the economies of the countries parties to such agreements. They also recognize that the purpose of a customs union or of a free-trade area should be to facilitate trade between the constituent territories and not to raise barriers to the trade of other contracting parties with such territories.

5. Accordingly, the provisions of this Agreement shall not prevent, as between the territories of contracting parties, the formation of a customs union or of a free-trade area or the adoption of an interim agreement necessary for the formation of a customs union or of a free-trade area; *provided* that:

   (*a*) with respect to a customs union, or an interim agreement leading to a formation of a customs union, the duties and other regulations of commerce imposed at the institution of any such union or interim agreement in respect of trade with contracting parties not parties to such union or agreement shall not on the whole be higher or more restrictive than the general incidence of the duties and regulations of commerce applicable in the constituent territories prior to the formation of such union or the adoption of such interim agreement, as the case may be;

(*b*) with respect to a free-trade area, or an interim agreement leading to the formation of a free-trade area, the duties and other regulations of commerce maintained in each of the constituent territories and applicable at the formation of such free-trade area or the adoption of such interim agreement to the trade of contracting parties not included in such area or not parties to such agreement shall not be higher or more restrictive than the corresponding duties and other regulations of commerce existing in the same constituent territories prior to the formation of the free-trade area, or interim agreement as the case may be; and

(*c*) any interim agreement referred to in sub-paragraphs (a) and (b) shall include a plan and schedule for the formation of such a customs union or of such a free-trade area within a reasonable length of time.

6. If, in fulfilling the requirements of sub-paragraph 5 (a), a contracting party proposes to increase any rate of duty inconsistently with the provisions of Article II, the procedure set forth in Article XXVIII shall apply. In providing for compensatory adjustment, due account shall be

taken of the compensation already afforded by the reduction brought about in the corresponding duty of the
other constituents of the union.

7. (a) Any contracting party deciding to enter into a customs union or free-trade area, or an interim agreement leading to the formation of such a union or
area, shall promptly notify the Contracting Parties
and shall make available to them such information
regarding the proposed union or area as will enable
them to make such reports and recommendations to
contracting parties as they may deem appropriate.

(b) If, after having studied the plan and schedule included in an interim agreement referred to in paragraph 5 in consultation with the parties to that
agreement and taking due account of the information made available in accordance with the provisions of sub-paragraph (a), the Contracting Parties
find that such agreement is not likely to result in the
formation of a customs union or of a free-trade area
within the period contemplated by the parties to the
agreement or that such period is not a reasonable
one, the Contracting Parties shall make recommendations to the parties to the agreement. The parties
shall not maintain or put into force, as the case may

be, such agreement if they are not prepared to modify it in accordance with these recommendations.

(c) Any substantial change in the plan or schedule referred to in paragraph 5 (c) shall be communicated to the Contracting Parties, which may request the contracting parties concerned to consult with them if the change seems likely to jeopardize or delay unduly the formation of the customs union or of the free-trade area.

8. For the purposes of this Agreement:

(a) A customs union shall be understood to mean the substitution of a single customs territory for two or more customs territories, so that

(i) duties and other restrictive regulations of commerce (except, where necessary, those permitted under Articles XI, XII, XIII, XIV, XV, and XX) are eliminated with respect to substantially all the trade between the constituent territories of the union or at least with respect to substantially all the trade in products originating in such territories, and,

(ii) subject to the provisions of paragraph 9, substantially the same duties and other regulations of commerce are applied by each of the members of the union to the trade of territories not included in the union.

(*b*) A free-trade area shall be understood to mean a group of two or more customs territories in which the duties and other restrictive regulations of commerce (except, where necessary, those permitted under Articles XI, XII, XIII, XIV, XV, and XX) are eliminated on substantially all the trade between the constituent territories in products originating in such territories.

9. The preferences referred to in paragraph 2 of Article I shall not be affected by the formation of a customs union or of a free-trade area but may be eliminated or adjusted by means of negotiations with contracting parties affected.* This procedure of negotiations with affected contracting parties shall, in particular, apply to the elimination of preferences required to conform with the provisions of paragraph 8 (a)(i) and paragraph 8 (b).

10. The Contracting Parties may by a two-thirds majority approve proposals which do not fully comply with the requirements of paragraphs 5 to 9 inclusive, provided that such proposals lead to the formation of a customs union or a free-trade area in the sense of this Article.

11. Taking into account the exceptional circumstances aris-
    ing out of the establishment of India and Pakistan as
    independent States and recognizing the fact that they
    have long constituted an economic unit, the contract-
    ing parties agree that the provisions of this Agreement
    shall not prevent the two countries from entering into
    special arrangements with respect to the trade between
    them, pending the establishment of their mutual trade
    relations on a definitive basis.*

12. Each contracting party shall take such reasonable mea-
    sures as may be available to it to ensure observance of
    the provisions of this Agreement by the regional and
    local governments and authorities within its territories.

## Ad Article XXIV

*Paragraph 9*

It is understood that the provisions of Article I would require
that, when a product which has been imported into the territory of a member of a customs union or free-trade area
at a preferential rate of duty is re-exported to the territory
of another member of such union or area, the latter member should collect a duty equal to the difference between
the duty already paid and any higher duty that would be

payable if the product were being imported directly into its territory.

*Paragraph 11*

Measures adopted by India and Pakistan in order to carry out definitive trade arrangements between them, once they have been agreed upon, might depart from particular provisions of this Agreement, but these measures would in general be consistent with the objectives of the Agreement.

# Understanding on the Interpretation of Article XXIV of the General Agreement on Tariffs and Trade 1994

*Members,*

*Having regard* to the provisions of Article XXIV of GATT 1994;

*Recognizing* that customs unions and free-trade areas have greatly increased in number and importance since the establishment of GATT 1947 and today cover a significant proportion of world trade;

*Recognizing* the contribution to the expansion of world trade that may be made by closer integration between the economies of the parties to such agreements;

Appendices

*Recognizing* also that such contribution is increased if the elimination between the constituent territories of duties and other restrictive regulations of commerce extends to all trade, and diminished if any major sector of trade is excluded;

*Reaffirming* that the purpose of such agreements should be to facilitate trade between the constituent territories and not to raise barriers to the trade of other Members with such territories; and that in their formation or enlargement the parties to them should to the greatest possible extent avoid creating adverse effects on the trade of other Members;

*Convinced* also of the need to reinforce the effectiveness of the role of the Council for Trade in Goods in reviewing agreements notified under Article XXIV, by clarifying the criteria and procedures for the assessment of new or enlarged agreements, and improving the transparency of all Article XXIV agreements;

*Recognizing* the need for a common understanding of the obligations of Members under paragraph 12 of Article XXIV;

Hereby *agree* as follows:

1. Customs unions, free-trade areas, and interim agreements leading to the formation of a customs union or

free-trade area, to be consistent with Article XXIV, must satisfy, inter alia, the provisions of paragraphs 5, 6, 7, and 8 of that Article.

*Article XXIV:5*

2. The evaluation under paragraph 5(a) of Article XXIV of the general incidence of the duties and other regulations of commerce applicable before and after the formation of a customs union shall in respect of duties and charges be based upon an overall assessment of weighted average tariff rates and of customs duties collected. This assessment shall be based on import statistics for a previous representative period to be supplied by the customs union, on a tariff-line basis and in values and quantities, broken down by WTO country of origin. The Secretariat shall compute the weighted average tariff rates and customs duties collected in accordance with the methodology used in the assessment of tariff offers in the Uruguay Round of Multilateral Trade Negotiations. For this purpose, the duties and charges to be taken into consideration shall be the applied rates of duty. It is recognized that for the purpose of the overall assessment of the incidence of other regulations of commerce for which quantification and aggregation are

difficult, the examination of individual measures, regulations, products covered and trade flows affected may be required.

3. The "reasonable length of time" referred to in paragraph 5(c) of Article XXIV should exceed 10 years only in exceptional cases. In cases where Members parties to an interim agreement believe that 10 years would be insufficient, they shall provide a full explanation to the Council for Trade in Goods of the need for a longer period.

*Article XXIV:6*

4. Paragraph 6 of Article XXIV establishes the procedure to be followed when a Member forming a customs union proposes to increase a bound rate of duty. In this regard, Members reaffirm that the procedure set forth in Article XXVIII, as elaborated in the guidelines adopted on 10 November 1980 (BISD 27S/26-28) and in the Understanding on the Interpretation of Article XXVIII of GATT 1994, must be commenced before tariff concessions are modified or withdrawn upon the formation of a customs union or an interim agreement leading to the formation of a customs union.

5. These negotiations will be entered into in good faith with a view to achieving mutually satisfactory

compensatory adjustment. In such negotiations, as required by paragraph 6 of Article XXIV, due account shall be taken of reductions of duties on the same tariff line made by other constituents of the customs union upon its formation. Should such reductions not be sufficient to provide the necessary compensatory adjustment, the customs union would offer compensation, which may take the form of reductions of duties on other tariff lines. Such an offer shall be taken into consideration by the Members having negotiating rights in the binding being modified or withdrawn. Should the compensatory adjustment remain unacceptable, negotiations should be continued. Where, despite such efforts, agreement in negotiations on compensatory adjustment under Article XXVIII as elaborated by the Understanding on the Interpretation of Article XXVIII of GATT 1994 cannot be reached within a reasonable period from the initiation of negotiations, the customs union shall, nevertheless, be free to modify or withdraw the concessions; affected Members shall then be free to withdraw substantially equivalent concessions in accordance with Article XXVIII.

6. GATT 1994 imposes no obligation on Members benefiting from a reduction of duties consequent upon the

formation of a customs union, or an interim agreement leading to the formation of a customs union, to provide compensatory adjustment to its constituents.

*Review of Customs Unions and Free-Trade Areas*

7. All notifications made under paragraph 7(a) of Article XXIV shall be examined by a working party in the light of the relevant provisions of GATT 1994 and of paragraph 1 of this Understanding. The working party shall submit a report to the Council for Trade in Goods on its findings in this regard. The Council for Trade in Goods may make such recommendations to Members as it deems appropriate.

8. In regard to interim agreements, the working party may in its report make appropriate recommendations on the proposed time-frame and on measures required to complete the formation of the customs union or free-trade area. It may, if necessary, provide for further review of the agreement.

9. Members parties to an interim agreement shall notify substantial changes in the plan and schedule included in that agreement to the Council for Trade in Goods and, if so requested, the Council shall examine the changes.

10. Should an interim agreement notified under paragraph 7(a) of Article XXIV not include a plan and schedule, contrary to paragraph 5(c) of Article XXIV, the working party shall in its report recommend such a plan and schedule. The parties shall not maintain or put into force, as the case may be, such agreement if they are not prepared to modify it in accordance with these recommendations. Provision shall be made for subsequent review of the implementation of the recommendations.

11. Customs unions and constituents of free-trade areas shall report periodically to the Council for Trade in Goods, as envisaged by the CONTRACTING PARTIES to GATT 1947 in their instruction to the GATT 1947 Council concerning reports on regional agreements (BISD 18S/38), on the operation of the relevant agreement. Any significant changes and/or developments in the agreements should be reported as they occur.

*Dispute Settlement*

12. The provisions of Articles XXII and XXIII of GATT 1994 as elaborated and applied by the Dispute Settlement Understanding may be invoked with respect to any matters arising from the application of those provisions of Article XXIV relating to customs unions, free-trade areas, or

interim agreements leading to the formation of a customs union or free-trade area.

*Article XXIV:12*

13. Each Member is fully responsible under GATT 1994 for the observance of all provisions of GATT 1994, and shall take such reasonable measures as may be available to it to ensure such observance by regional and local governments and authorities within its territory.

14. The provisions of Articles XXII and XXIII of GATT 1994 as elaborated and applied by the Dispute Settlement Understanding may be invoked in respect of measures affecting its observance taken by regional or local governments or authorities within the territory of a Member. When the Dispute Settlement Body has ruled that a provision of GATT 1994 has not been observed, the responsible Member shall take such reasonable measures as may be available to it to ensure its observance. The provisions relating to compensation and suspension of concessions or other obligations apply in cases where it has not been possible to secure such observance.

15. Each Member undertakes to accord sympathetic consideration to and afford adequate opportunity for consultation regarding any representations made by another

Member concerning measures affecting the operation of
GATT 1994 taken within the territory of the former.

## Developing Country Exception

Decision of 28 November 1979 (L/4903)

Following negotiations within the framework of the Multilateral Trade Negotiations, the CONTRACTING PARTIES de-
cide as follows:

1. Notwithstanding the provisions of Article I of the General Agreement, contracting parties may accord differential and more favorable treatment to developing
   countries(*1*), without according such treatment to other
   contracting parties.
2. The provisions of paragraph 1 apply to the following (*2* ):
   *a*) Preferential tariff treatment accorded by developed
      contracting parties to products originating in devel-
      oping countries in accordance with the Generalized
      System of Preferences (*3*);
   *b*) Differential and more favorable treatment with re-
      spect to the provisions of the General Agreement
      concerning non-tariff measures governed by the

provisions of instruments multilaterally negotiated under the auspices of the GATT;

c) Regional or global arrangements entered into amongst less-developed contracting parties for the mutual reduction or elimination of tariffs and, in accordance with criteria or conditions which may be prescribed by the CONTRACTING PARTIES, for the mutual reduction or elimination of non-tariff measures, on products imported from one another;

d) Special treatment on the least developed among the developing countries in the context of any general or specific measures in favor of developing countries.

3. Any differential and more favorable treatment provided under this clause:

a) shall be designed to facilitate and promote the trade of developing countries and not to raise barriers to or create undue difficulties for the trade of any other contracting parties;

b) shall not constitute an impediment to the reduction or elimination of tariffs and other restrictions to trade on a most-favored-nation basis;

c) shall in the case of such treatment accorded by developed contracting parties to developing countries be designed and, if necessary, modified, to respond positively to the development, financial, and trade needs of developing countries.

4. Any contracting party taking action to introduce an arrangement pursuant to paragraphs 1, 2, and 3 above or subsequently taking action to introduce modification or withdrawal of the differential and more favorable treatment so provided shall:(4)

*a*) notify the CONTRACTING PARTIES and furnish them with all the information they may deem appropriate relating to such action;

*b*) afford adequate opportunity for prompt consultations at the request of any interested contracting party with respect to any difficulty or matter that may arise. The CONTRACTING PARTIES shall, if requested to do so by such contracting party, consult with all contracting parties concerned with respect to the matter with a view to reaching solutions satisfactory to all such contracting parties.

5. The developed countries do not expect reciprocity for commitments made by them in trade negotiations to reduce or remove tariffs and other barriers to the trade of developing countries, i.e., the developed countries do not expect the developing countries, in the course of trade negotiations, to make contributions which are

inconsistent with their individual development, financial, and trade needs. Developed contracting parties shall therefore not seek, neither shall less-developed contracting parties be required to make, concessions that are inconsistent with the latter's development, financial, and trade needs.

6. Having regard to the special economic difficulties and the particular development, financial, and trade needs of the least-developed countries, the developed countries shall exercise the utmost restraint in seeking any concessions or contributions for commitments made by them to reduce or remove tariffs and other barriers to the trade of such countries, and the least-developed countries shall not be expected to make concessions or contributions that are inconsistent with the recognition of their particular situation and problems.

7. The concessions and contributions made and the obligations assumed by developed and less-developed contracting parties under the provisions of the General Agreement should promote the basic objectives of the Agreement, including those embodied in the Preamble and in Article XXXVI. Less-developed contracting parties expect that their capacity to make contributions or negotiated concessions or take other mutually agreed

action under the provisions and procedures of the General Agreement would improve with the progressive development of their economies and improvement in their trade situation and they would accordingly expect to participate more fully in the framework of rights and obligations under the General Agreement.

8. Particular account shall be taken of the serious difficulty of the least-developed countries in making concessions and contributions in view of their special economic situation and their development, financial, and trade needs.

9. The contracting parties will collaborate in arrangements for review of the operation of these provisions, bearing in mind the need for individual and joint efforts by contracting parties to meet the development needs of developing countries and the objectives of the General Agreement.

Source: http://www.wto.org

## 2.2. Preferential Trade Agreements Notified to the GATT/WTO and in Force

| Agreement | Date of entry into force | GATT/WTO notification | |
| --- | --- | --- | --- |
| | | Related provisions | Type of agreement |
| EC accession of Austria, Finland and Sweden | 1-Jan-95 | GATT Art. XXIV | Accession to customs union |
| EC accession of Portugal and Spain | 1-Jan-86 | GATT Art. XXIV | Accession to customs union |
| EC accession of Greece | 1-Jan-81 | GATT Art. XXIV | Accession to customs union |
| EC accession of Denmark, Ireland and United Kingdom | 1-Jan-73 | GATT Art. XXIV | Accession to customs union |
| CEFTA accession of Bulgaria | 1-Jan-99 | GATT Art. XXIV | Accession to free trade agreement |
| CEFTA accession of Romania | 1-Jul-97 | GATT Art. XXIV | Accession to free trade agreement |
| CEFTA accession of Slovenia | 1-Jan-96 | GATT Art. XXIV | Accession to free trade agreement |

|  | | GATT/WTO notification | |
| Agreement | Date of entry into force | Related provisions | Type of agreement |
| --- | --- | --- | --- |
| EFTA accession of Iceland | 1-Mar-70 | GATT Art. XXIV | Accession to free trade agreement |
| EC accession of Austria, Finland and Sweden | 1-Jan-95 | GATS Art. V | Accession to services agreement |
| EAEC | 8-Oct-97 | GATT Art. XXIV | Customs union |
| EC – Andorra | 1-Jul-91 | GATT Art. XXIV | Customs union |
| EC – Turkey | 1-Jan-96 | GATT Art. XXIV | Customs union |
| Czech Republic – Slovak Republic | 1-Jan-93 | GATT Art. XXIV | Customs union |
| MERCOSUR | 29-Nov-91 | Enabling Clause | Customs union |
| CARICOM | 1-Aug-73 | GATT Art. XXIV | Customs union |
| EC – Cyprus | 1-Jun-73 | GATT Art. XXIV | Customs union |
| EC – Malta | 1-Apr-71 | GATT Art. XXIV | Customs union |

*(continued)*

| Agreement | Date of entry into force | GATT/WTO notification | |
| --- | --- | --- | --- |
| | | Related provisions | Type of agreement |
| CACM | 12-Oct-61 | GATT Art. XXIV | Customs union |
| EC (Treaty of Rome) | 1-Jan-58 | GATT Art. XXIV | Customs union |
| Bulgaria – Lithuania | 1-Mar-02 | GATT Art. XXIV | Free trade agreement |
| Bulgaria – Israel | 1-Jan-02 | GATT Art. XXIV | Free trade agreement |
| Bulgaria – Latvia | 1-Apr-03 | GATT Art. XXIV | Free trade agreement |
| Bulgaria – Estonia | 1-Jan-02 | GATT Art. XXIV | Free trade agreement |
| EFTA – Singapore | 1-Jan-03 | GATT Art. XXIV | Free trade agreement |
| Canada – Costa Rica | 1-Nov-02 | GATT Art. XXIV | Free trade agreement |
| EC – Croatia | 1-Mar-02 | GATT Art. XXIV | Free trade agreement |
| EC – Jordan | 1-May-02 | GATT Art. XXIV | Free trade agreement |
| Japan – Singapore | 30-Nov-02 | GATT Art. XXIV | Free trade agreement |

# Appendices

| Agreement | Date of entry into force | GATT/WTO notification Related provisions | Type of agreement |
|---|---|---|---|
| India – Sri Lanka | 15-Dec-01 | Enabling Clause | Free trade agreement |
| Chile – Costa Rica | 15-Feb-02 | GATT Art. XXIV | Free trade agreement |
| Turkey – Slovenia | 1-Jun-00 | GATT Art. XXIV | Free trade agreement |
| United States – Jordan | 17-Dec-01 | GATT Art. XXIV | Free trade agreement |
| EFTA – Jordan | 1-Jan-02 | GATT Art. XXIV | Free trade agreement |
| EFTA – Croatia | 1-Jan-02 | GATT Art. XXIV | Free trade agreement |
| Slovenia – Bosnia and Herzegovina | 1-Jan-02 | GATT Art. XXIV | Free trade agreement |
| EC – FYROM | 1-Jun-01 | GATT Art. XXIV | Free trade agreement |
| Hungary – Estonia | 1-Mar-01 | GATT Art. XXIV | Free trade agreement |
| New Zealand – Singapore | 1-Jan-01 | GATT Art. XXIV | Free trade agreement |
| EFTA – Mexico | 1-Jul-01 | GATT Art. XXIV | Free trade agreement |

(*continued*)

Appendices

| Agreement | Date of entry into force | GATT/WTO notification | |
| | | Related provisions | Type of agreement |
| --- | --- | --- | --- |
| Chile – Mexico | 1-Aug-99 | GATT Art. XXIV | Free trade agreement |
| Mexico – Israel | 1-Jul-00 | GATT Art. XXIV | Free trade agreement |
| Georgia – Armenia | 11-Nov-98 | GATT Art. XXIV | Free trade agreement |
| Georgia – Azerbaijan | 10-Jul-96 | GATT Art. XXIV | Free trade agreement |
| Georgia – Kazakhstan | 16-Jul-99 | GATT Art. XXIV | Free trade agreement |
| Georgia – Russian Federation | 10-May-94 | GATT Art. XXIV | Free trade agreement |
| Georgia – Turkmenistan | 1-Jan-00 | GATT Art. XXIV | Free trade agreement |
| Georgia – Ukraine | 4-Jun-96 | GATT Art. XXIV | Free trade agreement |
| EFTA – Former Yugoslav Republic of Macedonia | 1-Jan-01 | GATT Art. XXIV | Free trade agreement |
| Latvia – Turkey | 1-Jul-00 | GATT Art. XXIV | Free trade agreement |

| Agreement | Date of entry into force | GATT/WTO notification Related provisions | Type of agreement |
|---|---|---|---|
| Turkey – Former Yugoslav Republic of Macedonia | 1-Sep-00 | GATT Art. XXIV | Free trade agreement |
| Kyrgyz Republic – Armenia | 27-Oct-95 | GATT Art. XXIV | Free trade agreement |
| EC – South Africa | 1-Jan-00 | GATT Art. XXIV | Free trade agreement |
| EC – Morocco | 1-Mar-00 | GATT Art. XXIV | Free trade agreement |
| EC – Israel | 1-Jun-00 | GATT Art. XXIV | Free trade agreement |
| EC – Mexico | 1-Jul-00 | GATT Art. XXIV | Free trade agreement |
| Estonia – Ukraine | 14-Mar-96 | GATT Art. XXIV | Free trade agreement |
| Poland – Turkey | 1-May-00 | GATT Art. XXIV | Free trade agreement |
| EFTA – Morocco | 1-Dec-99 | GATT Art. XXIV | Free trade agreement |
| Bulgaria – Former Yugoslav Republic of Macedonia | 1-Jan-00 | GATT Art. XXIV | Free trade agreement |

(*continued*)

| Agreement | Date of entry into force | GATT/WTO notification | |
| --- | --- | --- | --- |
| | | Related provisions | Type of agreement |
| Hungary – Latvia | 1-Jan-00 | GATT Art. XXIV | Free trade agreement |
| Hungary – Lithuania | 1-Mar-00 | GATT Art. XXIV | Free trade agreement |
| CIS | 30-Dec-94 | GATT Art. XXIV | Free trade agreement |
| Kyrgyz Republic – Kazakhstan | 11-Nov-95 | GATT Art. XXIV | Free trade agreement |
| Poland – Latvia | 1-Jun-99 | GATT Art. XXIV | Free trade agreement |
| EFTA – Palestinian Authority | 1-Jul-99 | GATT Art. XXIV | Free trade agreement |
| Poland – Faroe Islands | 1-Jun-99 | GATT Art. XXIV | Free trade agreement |
| BAFTA | 1-Apr-94 | GATT Art. XXIV | Free trade agreement |
| Kyrgyz Republic – Moldova | 21-Nov-96 | GATT Art. XXIV | Free trade agreement |
| Kyrgyz Republic – Russian Federation | 24-Apr-93 | GATT Art. XXIV | Free trade agreement |
| Kyrgyz Republic – Ukraine | 19-Jan-98 | GATT Art. XXIV | Free trade agreement |

| Agreement | Date of entry into force | GATT/WTO notification | |
| --- | --- | --- | --- |
| | | Related provisions | Type of agreement |
| Kyrgyz Republic – Uzbekistan | 20-Mar-98 | GATT Art. XXIV | Free trade agreement |
| Bulgaria – Turkey | 1-Jan-99 | GATT Art. XXIV | Free trade agreement |
| Czech Republic – Turkey | 1-Sep-98 | GATT Art. XXIV | Free trade agreement |
| Slovak Republic – Turkey | 1-Sep-98 | GATT Art. XXIV | Free trade agreement |
| EC – Tunisia | 1-Mar-98 | GATT Art. XXIV | Free trade agreement |
| Estonia – Turkey | 1-Jun-98 | GATT Art. XXIV | Free trade agreement |
| Slovenia – Israel | 1-Sep-98 | GATT Art. XXIV | Free trade agreement |
| Poland – Israel | 1-Mar-98 | GATT Art. XXIV | Free trade agreement |
| Estonia – Faroe Islands | 1-Dec-98 | GATT Art. XXIV | Free trade agreement |
| Czech Republic – Estonia | 12-Feb-98 | GATT Art. XXIV | Free trade agreement |

(*continued*)

Appendices

| Agreement | Date of entry into force | GATT/WTO notification | |
| --- | --- | --- | --- |
| | | Related provisions | Type of agreement |
| Slovak Republic – Estonia | 12-Feb-98 | GATT Art. XXIV | Free trade agreement |
| Lithuania – Turkey | 1-Mar-98 | GATT Art. XXIV | Free trade agreement |
| Israel – Turkey | 1-May-97 | GATT Art. XXIV | Free trade agreement |
| Romania – Turkey | 1-Feb-98 | GATT Art. XXIV | Free trade agreement |
| Hungary – Turkey | 1-Apr-98 | GATT Art. XXIV | Free trade agreement |
| Czech Republic – Israel | 1-Dec-97 | GATT Art. XXIV | Free trade agreement |
| Slovak Republic – Israel | 1-Jan-97 | GATT Art. XXIV | Free trade agreement |
| Slovenia – Croatia | 1-Jan-98 | GATT Art. XXIV | Free trade agreement |
| Hungary – Israel | 1-Feb-98 | GATT Art. XXIV | Free trade agreement |
| Poland – Lithuania | 1-Jan-97 | GATT Art. XXIV | Free trade agreement |
| Slovak Republic – Latvia | 1-Jul-97 | GATT Art. XXIV | Free trade agreement |

Appendices

| | Date of entry into force | GATT/WTO notification | |
|---|---|---|---|
| Agreement | | Related provisions | Type of agreement |
| Slovak Republic – Lithuania | 1-Jul-97 | GATT Art. XXIV | Free trade agreement |
| Czech Republic – Latvia | 1-Jul-97 | GATT Art. XXIV | Free trade agreement |
| Czech Republic – Lithuania | 1-Sep-97 | GATT Art. XXIV | Free trade agreement |
| Romania – Moldova | 1-Jan-95 | GATT Art. XXIV | Free trade agreement |
| Canada – Chile | 5-Jul-97 | GATT Art. XXIV | Free trade agreement |
| EC – Palestinian Authority | 1-Jul-97 | GATT Art. XXIV | Free trade agreement |
| Slovenia – Estonia | 1-Jan-97 | GATT Art. XXIV | Free trade agreement |
| Slovenia – Former Yugoslav Republic of Macedonia | 1-Sep-96 | GATT Art. XXIV | Free trade agreement |
| Slovenia – Latvia | 1-Aug-96 | GATT Art. XXIV | Free trade agreement |

*(continued)*

| Agreement | Date of entry into force | GATT/WTO notification | |
| | | Related provisions | Type of agreement |
| --- | --- | --- | --- |
| Slovenia – Lithuania | 1-Mar-97 | GATT Art. XXIV | Free trade agreement |
| EC – Faroe Islands | 1-Jan-97 | GATT Art. XXIV | Free trade agreement |
| Canada – Israel | 1-Jan-97 | GATT Art. XXIV | Free trade agreement |
| EC – Slovenia | 1-Jan-97 | GATT Art. XXIV | Free trade agreement |
| EFTA – Estonia | 1-Jun-96 | GATT Art. XXIV | Free trade agreement |
| EFTA – Latvia | 1-Jun-96 | GATT Art. XXIV | Free trade agreement |
| EFTA – Lithuania | 1-Aug-96 | GATT Art. XXIV | Free trade agreement |
| EC – Czech Republic | 1-Mar-92 | GATT Art. XXIV | Free trade agreement |
| EC – Slovak Republic | 1-Mar-92 | GATT Art. XXIV | Free trade agreement |
| Faroe Islands – Norway | 1-Jul-93 | GATT Art. XXIV | Free trade agreement |
| Faroe Islands – Switzerland | 1-Mar-95 | GATT Art. XXIV | Free trade agreement |
| Faroe Islands – Iceland | 1-Jul-93 | GATT Art. XXIV | Free trade agreement |

Appendices

| Agreement | Date of entry into force | GATT/WTO notification | |
|---|---|---|---|
| | | Related provisions | Type of agreement |
| EFTA – Slovenia | 1-Jul-95 | GATT Art. XXIV | Free trade agreement |
| EC – Lithuania | 1-Jan-95 | GATT Art. XXIV | Free trade agreement |
| EC – Estonia | 1-Jan-95 | GATT Art. XXIV | Free trade agreement |
| EC – Latvia | 1-Jan-95 | GATT Art. XXIV | Free trade agreement |
| EC – Bulgaria | 31-Dec-93 | GATT Art. XXIV | Free trade agreement |
| EC – Romania | 1-May-93 | GATT Art. XXIV | Free trade agreement |
| CEFTA | 1-Mar-93 | GATT Art. XXIV | Free trade agreement |
| EFTA – Hungary | 1-Oct-93 | GATT Art. XXIV | Free trade agreement |
| EFTA – Poland | 15-Nov-93 | GATT Art. XXIV | Free trade agreement |
| EFTA – Bulgaria | 1-Jul-93 | GATT Art. XXIV | Free trade agreement |
| EFTA – Romania | 1-May-93 | GATT Art. XXIV | Free trade agreement |

(*continued*)

# Appendices

| Agreement | Date of entry into force | GATT/WTO notification | |
| --- | --- | --- | --- |
| | | Related provisions | Type of agreement |
| NAFTA | 1-Jan-94 | GATT Art. XXIV | Free trade agreement |
| EFTA – Israel | 1-Jan-93 | GATT Art. XXIV | Free trade agreement |
| EFTA – Czech Republic | 1-Jul-92 | GATT Art. XXIV | Free trade agreement |
| EFTA – Slovak Republic | 1-Jul-92 | GATT Art. XXIV | Free trade agreement |
| EC – Hungary | 1-Mar-92 | GATT Art. XXIV | Free trade agreement |
| EC – Poland | 1-Mar-92 | GATT Art. XXIV | Free trade agreement |
| EFTA – Turkey | 1-Apr-92 | GATT Art. XXIV | Free trade agreement |
| United States – Israel | 19-Aug-85 | GATT Art. XXIV | Free trade agreement |
| CER | 1-Jan-83 | GATT Art. XXIV | Free trade agreement |
| EC – Egypt | 1-Jul-77 | GATT Art. XXIV | Free trade agreement |
| EC – Lebanon | 1-Jul-77 | GATT Art. XXIV | Free trade agreement |

| Agreement | Date of entry into force | GATT/WTO notification | |
|---|---|---|---|
| | | Related provisions | Type of agreement |
| EC – Syria | 1-Jul-77 | GATT Art. XXIV | Free trade agreement |
| PATCRA | 1-Feb-77 | GATT Art. XXIV | Free trade agreement |
| EC – Algeria | 1-Jul-76 | GATT Art. XXIV | Free trade agreement |
| EC – Norway | 1-Jul-73 | GATT Art. XXIV | Free trade agreement |
| EC – Iceland | 1-Apr-73 | GATT Art. XXIV | Free trade agreement |
| EC – Switzerland and Liechtenstein | 1-Jan-73 | GATT Art. XXIV | Free trade agreement |
| EC – OCTs | 1-Jan-71 | GATT Art. XXIV | Free trade agreement |
| EFTA (Stockholm Convention) | 3-May-60 | GATT Art. XXIV | Free trade agreement |
| EAC | 7-Jul-00 | Enabling Clause | Other |
| CEMAC | 24-Jun-99 | Enabling Clause | Other |
| WAEMU/UEMOA | 1-Jan-00 | Enabling Clause | Other |
| MSG | 22-Jul-93 | Enabling Clause | Other |

(*continued*)

| Agreement | Date of entry into force | GATT/WTO notification | |
| | | Related provisions | Type of agreement |
| --- | --- | --- | --- |
| COMESA | 8-Dec-94 | Enabling Clause | Other |
| SAPTA | 7-Dec-95 | Enabling Clause | Other |
| AFTA | 28-Jan-92 | Enabling Clause | Other |
| CAN | 25-May-88 | Enabling Clause | Other |
| ECO | not available | Enabling Clause | Other |
| Laos – Thailand | 20-Jun-91 | Enabling Clause | Other |
| GCC | not available | Enabling Clause | Other |
| LAIA | 18-Mar-81 | Enabling Clause | Other |
| SPARTECA | 1-Jan-81 | Enabling Clause | Other |
| Bangkok Agreement | 17-Jun-76 | Enabling Clause | Other |
| GSTP | 19-Apr-89 | Enabling Clause | Other |
| PTN | 11-Feb-73 | Enabling Clause | Other |
| TRIPARTITE | 1-Apr-68 | Enabling Clause | Other |
| CARICOM | 1-Jul-97 | GATS Art. V | Services agreement |
| EFTA – Singapore | 1-Jan-03 | GATS Art. V | Services agreement |
| EFTA | 1-Jun-02 | GATS Art. V | Services agreement |

Appendices

| | | GATT/WTO notification | |
|---|---|---|---|
| Agreement | Date of entry into force | Related provisions | Type of agreement |
| Japan – Singapore | 30-Nov-02 | GATS Art. V | Services agreement |
| United States – Jordan | 17-Dec-01 | GATS Art. V | Services agreement |
| EC – Mexico | 1-Mar-01 | GATS Art. V | Services agreement |
| Chile – Costa Rica | 15-Feb-02 | GATS Art. V | Services agreement |
| EC – Slovenia | 1-Feb-99 | GATS Art. V | Services agreement |
| EC – Lithuania | 1-Feb-98 | GATS Art. V | Services agreement |
| EC – Estonia | 1-Feb-98 | GATS Art. V | Services agreement |
| EC – Latvia | 1-Feb-99 | GATS Art. V | Services agreement |
| New Zealand – Singapore | 1-Jan-01 | GATS Art. V | Services agreement |
| EFTA – Mexico | 1-Jul-01 | GATS Art. V | Services agreement |
| Chile – Mexico | 1-Aug-99 | GATS Art. V | Services agreement |

(*continued*)

| Agreement | Date of entry into force | GATT/WTO notification | |
| | | Related provisions | Type of agreement |
| --- | --- | --- | --- |
| Canada – Chile | 5-Jul-97 | GATS Art. V | Services agreement |
| EC – Bulgaria | 1-Feb-95 | GATS Art. V | Services agreement |
| EEA | 1-Jan-94 | GATS Art. V | Services agreement |
| EC – Czech Republic | 1-Feb-95 | GATS Art. V | Services agreement |
| EC – Romania | 1-Feb-95 | GATS Art. V | Services agreement |
| EC – Hungary | 1-Feb-94 | GATS Art. V | Services agreement |
| EC – Poland | 1-Feb-94 | GATS Art. V | Services agreement |
| EC – Slovak Republic | 1-Feb-95 | GATS Art. V | Services agreement |
| CER | 1-Jan-89 | GATS Art. V | Services agreement |
| EC (Treaty of Rome) | 1-Jan-58 | GATS Art. V | Services agreement |
| NAFTA | 1-Apr-94 | GATS Art. V | Services agreement |

# Chapter 3

## 3.1 NAFTA Rules of Origin

We draw on LaNasa (1993) to offer a brief description of the NAFTA rules of origin. A product qualifies for preferential treatment under NAFTA if it passes one of the following five tests:

i. The product is wholly obtained or produced in the territory of one or more of the member countries.

ii. The product is produced entirely in the territory of one or more of the Parties exclusively from originating materials.

iii. If a product contains any materials not originating in North America, it is classified as a North American good if each non-originating material undergoes a change in tariff classification caused by production that occurs entirely within Canada, Mexico, or the United States. NAFTA defines the required change by reference to changes in the Harmonized Tariff Schedule (HTS). The HTS is an international standard that harmonizes tariff nomenclature worldwide. It classifies products according to a hierarchical framework that reflects increasing degrees of technical sophistication and economic effort.

The type and degree of change required depends on the type of product.

iv. If a non-originating part does not qualify under the change in tariff classification test because the tariff heading for it and the product crossing the border is the same, the product can still be treated as originating in North America if it meets the required regional value content test.

v. If a good fails all of the above tests, the product will be classified as North American if the non-originating material is *de minimis* – that is, less than 7 percent of the transaction value (price) or total cost of the good.

There are three cases in which a good that qualifies for North American origin can be disqualified from preferential treatment. First, the good is disqualified if after qualifying, it undergoes further processing outside North America. Second, mere dilution with water or another substance that does not materially alter the characteristics of the product does not count as a qualifying operation. Finally, any good undergoing any process, work, or pricing practice aimed at circumventing NAFTA's rules of origin is disqualified from preferential treatment.

Appendices

# Chapter 5

## 5.1 Welfare Analysis

Given the quasi-linear form of the aggregate utility function, welfare analysis can be conducted using the standard surplus measures.

World welfare $= W$

$= \Sigma_j \left( A_j Q_j - Q_j^2/2 \right) - c \Sigma_j Q_j$

$= \Sigma_j \left( (A_j - c) Q_j - Q_j^2/2 \right)$

Therefore,

$\dfrac{dW}{dQ_j} = ((A_j - c) - Q_j) > 0, \quad \text{using} \quad (A_j - c) > Q_j$

From (3), (4), and (5), it is easy to see that $Q_j$ is decreasing in tariffs; therefore, welfare increases with an increase in each $Q_j$. We, therefore, have welfare being maximized at global free trade.

## 5.2 Derivation of (8) and (9)

Consider the incentives for country $X$. Expanding the terms in (7) gives us

$$\left( {}_B q_x^x \right)^2 + \left( {}_B q_y^x \right)^2 > \left( q_x^x \right)^2 + \left( q_y^x \right)^2$$

—✢ 179 ✢—

This reduces to

$$\left(_Bq_x^x + q_x^x\right)\left(q_x^x - _Bq_x^x\right) < \left(_Bq_y^x + q_x^x\right)\left(_Bq_y^x - q_y^x\right)$$

From (2), we have

$$q_x^x - _Bq_x^x = \frac{n_y}{n+1}t \quad \text{and} \quad _Bq_y^x - q_y^x = \frac{1 + n_y + n_z}{n+1}t$$

Substituting these into the previous expression, we get condition (8); (9) can be entirely analogously derived.

## 5.3 Numerical Example

Example: Let $n_x = n_y = n_z = 1$. (10) and (11) can be rewritten as

$$2\alpha_x < 6\alpha_y - 6t$$

and

$$2\alpha_y < 6\alpha_x - 6t$$

Let $\alpha_x = \alpha_y/2$. The conditions translate into $\alpha_y > \frac{6t}{5}$ and $\alpha_y > 6t$, both of which clearly hold if $\alpha_y > 6t$.

## 5.4 Loci in Figure 5.1

To verify that the loci YY and XX shift in the manner indicated in Figure 5.1, note that (10), with equality, could be rewritten as

$$\alpha_y > \alpha_x f(n_z) + q(n_z)$$

where $f'(n_z) < 0$. This proves that the slope of XX shifts in the manner indicated. Also, (10) implies that with a larger $n_z$, the righthand side increases. Therefore, *ceteris paribus* for (10) to hold with equality, $\alpha_x$ has to increase. Therefore, XX shifts lower as shown.

## 5.5 Trade Diversion

To see that a larger number of firms from $Z$, $n_z$, implies greater trade diversion, note that from (2), $X$'s initial volume of imports from $Z$ equals $\frac{n_z}{n+1}(\alpha_x - (1+n_x)t)$. The volume of imports with a bilateral arrangement $= \frac{n_z}{n+1}(\alpha_x - (1+n_x+x_y)t)$. Thus, volume of trade diverted $= \frac{n_y n_z}{n+1}t$, which is increasing in $n_z$.

## 5.6 Numerical Example

Let $A_x = A_y = 10$ and $A_z = 10$. Let $c = 5$ and $n_x = n_y = n_z = 1$. Instead of assuming that producer profits exclusively determine government decisions, let us assume that governments maximize a weighted welfare function of the form

$$W = 0.45(CS + TR) + 0.55(PS)$$

where $CS$, $TR$, and $PS$ denote consumer surplus, tariff revenues, and producer surplus, respectively. Initial (non-discriminatory) tariffs can be derived by assuming that governments maximize the welfare function while taking the other countries' tariffs as given. Numerically simulating the model for the parameter values mentioned previously, we get initial tariff $t_x = t_y = 1.8$ and $t_z = 1.8$. Also, initial (weighted) welfare levels are $W_x = W_y = 5.07$ for $X$ and $Y$, respectively. With bilateral tariff reductions between $X$ and $Y$, the welfare levels are $_BW_x = {_B}W_y = 6.13$. With global free trade, $_MW_x = {_M}W_y = {_M}W_z = 5.74$. Although all three countries would have reduced tariffs multilaterally (because $_MW_x > W_x, {_M}W_y > W_y$ and $_MW_z > W_z$), once the bilateral arrangement is in place, $X$ and $Y$ would clearly not want to reduce tariffs multilaterally against $Z$ (because $_MW_x < {_B}W_x$ and $_MW_y < {_B}W_y$).

# References

Andriamananjara, S., 2002, "On the Size and Number of Preferential Trading Arrangements," *Journal of International Trade & Economic Development*, Vol. 11 (3) 279–95.

Armington, P., 1969, "A Theory of Demand for Products Distinguished by Place of Production," *IMF Staff Papers*, 26, 159–78.

Bagwell, K., and R. Staiger, 1997, "Multilateral Cooperation During the Formation of Free Trade Areas," *International Economic Review*.

Baldwin, R., 1995, "A Domino Theory of Regionalism," in *Expanding European Regionalism: The EU's New Members*, Baldwin, R., P. Haaparanta, and J. Kiander (eds.), Cambridge University Press, Cambridge, UK.

Baldwin, R., and A. Venables, 1995, "Regional Economic Integration," in Gene Grossman and Kenneth Rogoff, eds., *Handbook of International Economics*, Volume III, Elsevier Science BV.

Barnett, W., 1979, "The Theoretical Foundations of the Rotterdam Model," *Review of Economic Studies*, 46, 109–30.

Barnett, W., 1981, *Consumer Demand and Labor Supply: Goods, Monetary Assets, and Time*, North Holland: Amsterdam.

## References

Barten, A. P., 1966, "Evidence on Slutsky Conditions for Demand Equations," *Review of Economics and Statistics*, Volume 49, 77–84.

Becker, G., 1983, "A Theory of Competition Among Pressure Groups for Political Influence," *Quarterly Journal of Economics*, XCVII, 371–400.

Bhagwati, J., 1968, "Trade Liberalization Among LDCs, Trade Theory, and GATT Rules," in J. N. Wolfe (ed.), *Value, Capital, and Growth: Papers in Honor of Sir John Hicks*, Edinburgh: Edinburgh University Press, Chap. 2, 21–43.

Bhagwati, J., 1971, "Trade-Diverting Customs Unions and Welfare Improvement: A Clarification," *Economic Journal*, LXXXI, 580–7.

Bhagwati, J., 1993, "Regionalism and Multilateralism: An Overview," in Jaime deMelo and Arvind Panagariya (eds.), *New Dimensions in Regional Integration*, Cambridge University Press, Cambridge, UK.

Bhagwati, J., and T.N. Srinivasan, 1969, "Optimal Intervention to Achieve Non-Economic Objectives," *Review of Economic Studies*, 36 (1).

Bhagwati, J., and A. Panagariya, 1996, "Free Trade Areas or Free Trade? The Economics of Preferential Trade Areas," *American Enterprise Institute*, AEI Press, Washington, DC.

Bohara, A., K. Gawande, and P. Sanguinetti, 2004, "Trade Diversion and Declining Tariffs: Evidence from Mercosur," *Journal of International Economics*, 64, 65–88.

Bond, E., C. Syropoulos, and A. Winters, 2001, "Deepening of Regional Integration and Multilateral Trade Agreements," *Journal of International Economics*.

Bond, E., and C. Syropoulos, 1996, "The Size of Trading Blocs Market Power and World Welfare Effects," *Journal of International Economics*, Elsevier, 40 (3), 411–437, 5.

# References

Bowden, R., and D. Turkington, 1984, *Instrumental Variables*, Cambridge University Press, Cambridge, UK.

Brander, J., and P. Krugman, 1983, "A Reciprocal Dumping Model of International Trade," *Journal of International Economics*, 313–21.

Brown, D., and R. Stern, 1989, United States–Canada Bilateral Tariff Elimination: The Role of Product Differentiation and Market Structure," in Feenstra, Robert, ed., *Trade Policies for International Competitiveness*, University of Chicago Press.

Cadot, O., A. Estevadeordal, and A. Suwa-Eisenman, 2003, "Rules of Origin as Export Subsidies," *Working Paper*, Laboratoire d'Economie Appliquee, INRA.

Clements, K., A. Selvanathan, and S. Selvanathan, 1996, "Applied Demand Analysis: A Survey," *The Economic Record*, Vol. 72, No. 216, 63–81.

Cooper, C.A., and B.F. Massell, 1965, "Toward a General Theory of Customs Unions for Developing Countries," *Journal of Political Economy*, 73, 256–83.

Coopmans, T., and H. Uzawa, 1990, "Constancy and Constant Differences of Price Elasticities of Demand," in Chipman and McFadden (eds.), *Preferences, Uncertainty, and Optimality: Essays in Honor of Leonid Hurwicz*, Westview Press, Boulder, CO.

Dam, K., 1970, *The GATT: Law and International Economic Organization*, University of Chicago Press.

Deardorff, A., and R. Stern, 1994, "Multilateral Trade Negotiations and Preferential Trading Arrangements," in Alan Deardorff and Robert Stern (eds.), *Analytical and Negotiating Issues in the Global Trading System*, University of Michigan Press, Ann Arbor.

Deardorff, A., 1997, "Determinants of Bilateral Trade: Does Gravity Work in a Neoclassical World," in Frankel (ed.), *Regionalization of the World Economy*, NBER, University of Chicago Press.

References

Deaton, A., and J. Muellbauer, 1980a, "An Almost Ideal Demand System," *American Economic Review*, 70, 312–26.

Deaton, A., and J. Muellbauer, 1980b, *Economics and Consumer Behavior*, Cambridge University Press, Cambridge, UK.

Dixit, A., 1984, "International Trade Policy for Oligopolistic Industries," *The Economic Journal*, IVC, 1–16.

Dixit, A., 1986, "Comparative Statics for Oligopoly," *International Economic Review*, XXVII, 107–22.

Dixit, A., 1987, "Tariffs and Subsidies Under Oligopoly: The Case of the U.S. Automobile Industry," in H. Kierzkowski (ed.), *Protection and Competition in International Trade*, Basil Blackwell, Oxford.

Estevadeordal, A., 2000, "Negotiating Market Access in the Americas: The Case of NAFTA," *Journal of World Trade*.

Estevadeordal, A., and K. Suominen, 2003, "Rules of Origin: An Analytical World Map," Mimeo.

Ethier, W., 1997, Frank Graham Memorial Lecture, Princeton University, Princeton, NJ.

Findlay, R., and S. Wellisz, 1982, "Endogenous Tariffs, the Political Economy of Trade Restrictions, and Welfare," in J. Bhagwati (ed.), *Import Competition and Response*, National Bureau of Economic Research, University of Chicago Press.

Fisher, I., 1927, *The Making of Index Numbers*, Houghton Mifflin.

Frankel, J., E. Stein, and S. Wei, 1996, "Trading Blocs: The Natural, The Unnatural, and The Super Natural?," *Journal of Development Economics*, 47 (1), 61–95.

Frankel, J., 1997, *Regional Trading Blocs in the World Economic System*, Institute for International Economics, Washington, DC.

Freund, C., 2000, "Multilateralism and the Endogenous Formation of Preferential Trade Agreements," *Journal of International Economics*.

# References

Gawande, K., and P. Krishna, 2003, The Political Economy of Trade Policy: An Empirical Survey, in Choi and Harrigan eds., *Handbook of International Trade*, Basil Blackwell.

Geraci, V., and W. Prewo, 1982, "An Empirical Demand and Supply Model of Multilateral Trade," *Review of Economics and Statistics*, 432–41.

Goldstein, M., and M. Khan, 1978, "The Supply and Demand for Exports: A Simultaneous Approach," *Review of Economics and Statistics*, 275–86.

Goldstein, M., and M. Khan, 1984, "Income and Price Effects in International Trade," in Jones and Kenen (eds.), *Handbook of International Economics*, Volume II.

Grinols, E., 1981, "An Extension of the Kemp–Wan Theorem on the Formation of Customs Unions," *Journal of International Economics*, 11: 259–66.

Grossman, G., and E. Helpman, 1994, "Protection for Sale," *American Economic Review*, LXXXIV, 833–50.

Grossman, G., and E. Helpman, 1995, "The Politics of Free Trade Arrangements," *American Economic Review*, LXXXV, 667–90.

Hickman, B., and L. Lawrence, 1973, "Elasticities of Substitution and Export Demand in a World Trade Model," *European Economic Review*, 347–80.

Hummels, D., 1997, Comments on "Regionalization of World Trade and Currencies: Economics and Politics," in Frankel (ed.), *Regionalization of the World Economy*, NBER, University of Chicago Press.

Johnson, H., 1962, *Money, Trade, and Economic Growth*, Harvard University Press, Cambridge, MA.

Johnson, H. G., 1965, "An Economic Theory of Protectionism, Tariff Bargaining, and the Formation of Customs Unions," *Journal of Political Economy*, 73, 256–83.

# References

Kemp, M., 1964, *The Pure Theory of International Trade*, Prentice-Hall, NJ.

Kemp, M., and W. Henry, 1976, "An Elementary Proposition Concerning the Formation of Customs Unions," *Journal of International Economics*, 6, No. 1, 95–8.

Krishna, K., 2004, "Understanding Rules of Origin," forthcoming in *The Origin of Goods: Rules of Origin in Regional Trade Agreements*, A. Estevadeordal et al. (eds.), Oxford University Press.

Krishna, P., 1998, "Regionalism and Multilateralism: A Political Economy Approach," *Quarterly Journal of Economics*.

Krishna, P., 2003a, "Are Regional Trading Partners 'Natural'?," *Journal of Political Economy*.

Krishna, P., and A. Panagariya, 2000, "A Unification of Second-Best Results in International Trade," *Journal of International Economics*.

Krishna, P., and J. Bhagwati, 1997, "Necessarily Welfare-Improving Customs Unions with Industrialization Constraints: The Cooper–Massell–Johnson–Bhagwati Proposition,î *Japan and the World Economy*.

Krugman, P., 1991, "The Move to Free Trade Zones," in *Policy Implications of Trade and Currency Zones*, Federal Reserve Bank of Kansas City, 7–41.

Krugman, P., 1992, "Is Bilateralism Bad?," in E. Helpman and A. Razin (eds.), *International Trade and Trade Policy*. MIT Press, Cambridge, MA.

LaNasa, J.A., 1993, "Rules of Origin Under North American Free Trade Agreement: A Substantial Transformation into Objectively Transparent Protectionism," *Harvard International Law Journal*, 34 (2), 381–406.

Levy, P., 1997, "A Political Economic Analysis of Free Trade Arrangements," *American Economic Review*.

# References

Limao, N., 2004, "Preferential Trade Agreements as Stumbling Blocks for Multilateral Trade Liberalization: Evidence for the U.S.," *Discussion Paper* 4884, Center for Economic Policy Research, University of Maryland.

Lipsey, R., 1958, *The Theory of Customs Unions: A General Equilibrium Analysis,* University of London, Ph.D. Thesis.

Lipsey, R., 1960, "The Theory of Customs Unions: A General Survey," *Economic Journal,* 70, 498–513.

Lipsey, R., and Lancaster, K., 1957, "The General Theory of Second Best," *Review of Economic Studies.*

Marquez, J., 1991, "The Econometrics of Elasticities or the Elasticity of Econometrics: An Empirical Analysis of U.S. Imports," *International Finance Discussion Paper Number 396,* Board of Governors of the Federal Reserve, Washington, DC.

Marquez, J., 1994, "The Econometrics of Elasticities or the Elasticity of Econometrics: An Empirical Analysis of U.S. Imports," *Review of Economics and Statistics,* 471–81.

McLaren, J., 2002, "A Theory of Insidious Regionalism," *Quarterly Journal Economics* CXVII, 571–608.

McMillan, J., 1993, "Does Regional Integration Foster Open Trade? Economic Theory and GATT's Article XXIV," in Anderson and Blackhurst (eds.), *Regional Integration and the Global Trading System,* St. Martin's Press, New York.

McMillan, J., and E. McCann, 1980, "Welfare Effects in Customs Unions," *Economic Journal,* 91, 697–703.

Meade, J., 1955, *The Theory of Customs Unions,* Amsterdam.

Michaely, M., 1976, "The Assumptions of Jacob Viner's Theory of Customs Unions," *Journal of International Economics.*

Mitra, D., 1999, "Endogenous Lobby Formation and Endogenous Protection: A Long Run Model of Trade Policy Determination," *American Economic Review.*

# References

Mundell, R., 1964, "Tariff Preferences and the Terms of Trade," *Manchester School of Economic Studies*, 1–13.

Newey, W., 1986, "Linear Instrumental Variable Estimation of Limited Dependent Variable Models with Endogenous Explanatory Variables," *Journal of Econometrics*, 127–41, Amsterdam.

Norman, V., 1990, "Assessing Trade and Welfare Effects of Trade Liberalization: A Comparison of Alternative Approaches to CGE Modeling with Imperfect Competition," *European Economic Review*, 34, 725–51.

O'Halloran, S., 1994, *Politics, Process, and American Trade Policy*, University of Michigan Press, Ann Arbor.

Ohyama, M., 1972, "Trade and Welfare in General Equilibrium," *Keio Economic Studies*, 9, 37–73.

Olson, M., 1965, *The Logic of Collective Action: Public Goods and the Theory of Groups*, Harvard University Press, Cambridge, MA.

Panagariya, A., 1996, "The Meade Model of Preferential Trading: History, Analytics, and Policy Implications," in B. J. Cohen (ed.), *Essays in Honor of Peter Kenen*, Cambridge University Press, Cambridge, UK.

Panagariya, A., 1997, "Preferential Trading and the Myth of Natural Trading Partners," *Japan and the World Economy*.

Panagariya, A., 2000, "Preferential Trade Liberalization: The Traditional Theory and New Developments," *Journal of Economic Literature*.

Panagariya, A., and P. Krishna, 2002, "On Necessarily Welfare-Enhancing Free Trade Areas," *Journal of International Economics*.

Peltzman, S., 1976, "Toward a More General Theory of Regulation," *Journal of Law and Economics*, XVIIII, 211–48.

Phillips, P. C. B., 1983, "Exact Small Sample Theory in Simultaneous Equations Model," in Griliches and Intriligator (eds.), *Handbook of Econometrics*, Vol. I, Amsterdam.

# References

Samuelson, P., 1956, "Social Indifference Curves," *Quarterly Journal of Economics*, 70 (1), 1–22.

Schiff, M., and A. Winters, 2003, *Regional Integration and Development*, Oxford University Press.

Srinivasan, T.N., 1993, "Discussion on Regionalism versus Multilateralism: Analytical Notes," in A. Panagariya and J. De Melo (eds.), *New Dimensions in Regional Integration*, World Bank, Washington, DC.

Srinivasan, T. N., 1997, Comments on "Continental Trading Blocs: Are They Natural or Supernatural?," in Frankel (ed.), Regionalization of the World Economy, NBER, University of Chicago Press.

Srinivasan, T.N., I. Wooton, and J. Whalley, 1993, "Measuring the Effects of Regionalism on Trade and Welfare," in Anderson and Blackhurst (eds.), *Regional Integration and the Global Trading System*, St. Martin's Press, New York.

Stigler, G., 1971, "The Theory of Economic Regulation," *Bell Journal of Economic and Management Science*, 3–21.

Summers, L., 1991, "Regionalism and the World Trading System," in *Policy Implications of Trade and Currency Zones*, Federal Reserve Bank of Kansas City.

Theil, H., 1965, "The Information Approach to Demand Analysis," *Econometrica*, 33, 67–87.

Trefler, D., 1993, "Trade Liberalization and the Theory of Endogenous Protection: An Econometric Study of U.S. Import Policy," *Journal of Political Economy*, 101 (1), 138–60.

Vanek, J., 1965, *General Equilibrium of International Discrimination*, Harvard University Press, Cambridge, MA.

Viner, J., 1950, *The Customs Unions Issue*, Carnegie Endowment for International Peace, New York.

Winters, A., 1984, "British Imports of Manufactures and the Common Market," *Oxford Economic Papers*, 36 (1), 103–18.

# References

Winters, A., 1985, "Separability and the Modelling of International Economic Integration: UK Exports to Five Industrial Countries," *European Economic Review*, 27 (3), 335–53.

Winters, A., 1997, "Regionalism and the Rest of the World: The Irrelevance of the Kemp–Wan Theorem," *Oxford Economic Papers*.

Wonnacott, P., and M. Lutz, 1987, "Is There a Case for Free Trade Areas?," in Jeffrey Schott (ed.), *Free Trade Areas and U.S. Trade Policy*, Institute for International Economics, Washington, DC.

Wonnacott, P., and R. Wonnacott, 1981, "Is Unilateral Tariff Reduction Preferable to a Customs Union? The Curious Case of the Missing Foreign Tariffs," *American Economic Review*, LXXI, 704–14.

Yi, S.S., 1996, "Endogenous Formation of Customs Unions Under Imperfect Competition: Open Regionalism Is Good," *Journal of International Economics*, 41, 153–77.

# Index

# Index

# Index

Index

Index

Index